SELECTED

POEMS,

1969-1981

Richard Shelton
Selected Poems

1969-1981

University of Pittsburgh Press

Published by the University of Pittsburgh Press, Pittsburgh, Pa. 15260
Copyright © 1982, Richard Shelton
Feffer and Simons, Inc., London
Manufactured in the United States of America

Library of Congress Cataloging in Publication Data

Shelton, Richard, 1933–
   Selected poems, 1969–1981.

   (Pitt poetry series)
   I. Title.   II. Series.
PS3569.H39367A6   1982   811'.54   82-2680
ISBN 0-8229-3470-1   AACR2
ISBN 0-8229-5349-9 (pbk.)

Some of these poems originally appeared in the following periodicals: *American Poetry Review, The Antioch Review, Beyond Baroque, The Falcon, Field, Glassworks, The Goddard Journal, The Gramercy Review, Grilled Flowers, Harper's, The Iowa Review, Ironwood, Kayak, New Mexico Magazine, The Paris Review, Pebble, Sawtooth,* and *Westigan Review.*

"April" originally appeared in *Chicago Tribune Magazine.* "August" is reprinted from *Lillabulero.* "Letter to a Lost Friend" first appeared in *Lotus.* "The Stone Garden" is reprinted by permission from *National Forum: The Phi Kappa Phi Journal,* Vol. LX, No. 3 (Summer, 1980), p. 38. "The Fourteenth Anniversary," "How to Amuse a Stone," "Point of View," "Saturday Night at the Elk's Club," "Survival," and "The White Hotel" are reprinted courtesy of *Poetry.* "My Love" first appeared in *The Seneca Review.*

"Alone," "On Lake Pend Oreille," "The Prophets," "Connais-tu le Pays?" (1969); "New Year's Eve," "Valediction," "Reunion," "He Who Remains," "The Tattooed Desert" (1970); "Winter," "Requiem for Sonora," "Totem" (1971); "Seven Preludes to Silence," "San Juan's Day," "The Great Gulf," "Choose One from Among Them" (1972); "Comfort," "The Princes of Exile," "Sonora for Sale" (1973); "Five Lies About the Moon" (1975); "Mexico" (1976); "The Prophet" (1977); and "Territorial Rights" (1980) were copyrighted in the respective years shown by The New Yorker Magazine, Inc.

Journal of Return was published in 1969 by Kayak Press. *The Tattooed Desert* and *Of All the Dirty Words* were published by the University of Pittsburgh Press in 1971 and 1972, respectively. *Chosen Place* was published in 1975 by Best Cellar Press. *You Can't Have Everything* (1975) and *The Bus to Veracruz* (1978) were published in the respective years shown by the University of Pittsburgh Press.

*The publication of this book is supported by grants
from the National Endowment for the Arts
in Washington, D.C., a Federal agency,
and the Pennsylvania Council on the Arts.*

For Lois

CONTENTS

CONTENTS

CONTENTS

CONTENTS

From

Journal of Return

1969

We who are self-possessed
own nothing. Even our names
get up in the night and run away.

AND THE SCARS WILL BE COVERED

responsibility fell at my feet
like a dead bird
and I left it for the collectors of feathers

now I am leaving these words on sand
for the water
and when everything is gone
a voice will say
that's home
where two paths cross without speaking
where a lost shoe full of darkness
is curled up
under the roots of the snow

then I will point myself in the right direction
alone I hope
I was never much for company
and start off down an empty road
toward winter and a silence
which no one will ever repair

ALONE

what a word and I thought it would be
less disrespectful
old rotten tooth hanging on
there is no radius for this

so here I am
with the rusty motor of hope
sticking out of the sand like a dead arm
well it lasted
long enough it lasted until it was over

it ground the corn and did the dishes
and when it started to break down
where could I hide the pieces
with that repairman
looking at my uncouth hair
while I handed him tools always
the wrong one

now I can watch bushes
running their fingers over the legs
of strangers and say why not
let them have whatever
they get out of it

under the shadows are more
shadows and under those shadows
is nothing

I have my work to do
inventing new memories
and keeping verbs in the proper mood
somebody has to
and if I walk my defeated secrets
like a dog what's that to you
who left by way of the mirror
still believing that rain shows mercy

when how many times did I tell you
the fireflies are naked and cold
in the rags of their light

ON LAKE PEND OREILLE

All day the wind has made love
to the lake and tonight the water
takes up its bruises and moves
away to a safer distance.

I am listening for the small
sounds of another departure.

Summer is leaving
as if she could afford the trip.
She stands by the road
in her ragged coat and fumbles
for her keys in the darkness.

At her pathetic signal
the aristocracy of leaves
will begin to let go.

THE PROPHETS

I keep pushing this
wheelbarrow full of ambition
down a bruised road
toward blind decisions like roadsigns
in a language I cannot read

with my brother the general
and my frenzied companion
the inner voice I have come a long way

but the dead do not
wait they do not give a damn
about any of us

I search for their lost faces
in a field of broken mirrors and find
only my eyes shattered
as usual vacant as usual

and all this time the dead
know what they are doing
they attend classes in forgetting
and come out with diplomas of silence

from nests in their ripe mouths
the aisles of teeth open like wings
and fly away

I shout to them across the distance I
tell them the worst thing
that can happen has happened

but they rise out of themselves
laughing silently watching
their fingers drip from their hands
letting them go

SONORA

1

What do these mountains want?
Why do they rearrange themselves
and move silently closer at night?

They never sleep.

Sometimes I shout at them
that I am not afraid
and they absorb my voice.

Dawn comes to them from another country,
speaking a foreign tongue
to which they pay no attention.

2

I am faded by the moon
like pale nocturnal stones.
I come alive in the soft light of darkness.

The road extends a thin white hand
to lead me back. I cross it quickly
and move on through the desert.

Tonight I hear
the oriental voices
of coyotes
as if they have just learned
they were not supposed to be born.

They wail against silence,
and these constant stars
are more than anyone can bear
for very long.

3

Just after sunset
bats lurch through the sky
as if on broken wings.
Their voices are tiny and pitiful,
their faces masks of pain.
It is a ceremony
which causes the moon to rise.

4

A tarantula lumbers down the pale road
which he believes
was built for his convenience.
He loves to travel and is
untroubled by ideas
of time or destination.

5

Skeletons of saguaros
stand in amazement long after death
while the moon changes them
into designs of light and shadow
and their gray ribs
hold the wind in a dark circle
where it cries and circles,
circles and cries.

6

Night in this desert
is a great glass bell.
I have shouted against its walls
and there was no echo,
but the gods of Sonora heard me.

They sleep until the earth cools.
Then they walk down from the mountains
and shaggy-headed cholla
go to meet them.

I have never seen
the place where they meet,
but it is near.

7

After years of being watched
and listened to
I have learned to pray dark prayers.

Now I can anticipate
the scream of a rabbit,
and night birds fly through me
as if I were a shadow
thrown by the moon
over these faded stones.

8

The crow sits
on the stump of a blasted mesquite
where lightning has been.
He worships the god of fire
whose color is black.

He is aware of his sleek beauty
and slender yellow legs.

9

In this desert
each stone has its own name
and no two have the same name.
When I stand
between my shadow and the moon
I hear their unborn children
pushing up through dry sand.

I hear the firm clenching
of claws on branches
where birds sleep,
and I am aware of rabbits
listening for the shadow of an owl
whose eyes are always perfect circles.

No one knows what causes
lights which wander on the mountains
nor why certain shadows
have no agents.
It is more worthwhile
to contemplate the cholla's
luminous blond hair
or study night's great jeweled belly
for signs of dawn.

10

I came to this desert
from the north
where the god of water
lives in a silent blue house.

Now I am walking in the morning
and rain hangs from the sky.
I do not know this trail
nor where I am going,
but in the east
I see brightness lying down.

11

The voice of these mountains
is above the voice of thunder
and below the voice of the grasshopper.

They sing about a blue stone
whose home is in the south
and a black stone
whose home is in the north.
They sing about the shell
of many colors in the west
and the white shell
in the east.

12

Seven years ago I found these stones
scattered in the desert
and built a wall.
Now they are climbing down,
slowly sorting themselves
into families and going home.
Neither time nor distance
can discourage them,
and since I have seen
their subtle movements
I would not try to stop them.

Watching stones for seven years
has taught me little,
but it is enough.

And I am no longer afraid
of the saguaros.
They are overgrown children
swinging their arms,
grinning stupidly.
In the spring each wears
a large white flower on its head.
Their great green hearts are gentle,
and tiny owls nest in their eyes.

13

What were the lizards
before they shrank?
Were they huge monsters
or gods with fringed mouths?
Or were they both?

I have asked them many times
and they are always too sleepy
to answer. But in that second
before the film of sleep
comes over their eyes
I see the cold memory
of an earlier world below,
without sun or moon.

Their tiny arthritic hands
stretch out on warm stone.
They sleep. I will not stand
between them and the sun.

14

Tonight when I wade
through rivers of cold air
in black arroyos
the coyotes will be still
and listen.

The white coyote is good
and the yellow coyote is bad,
but each owl is the same owl
and all are holy.

15

Now dark cloud and his younger brother
let the rain down
as a curtain.
May it be happy behind me.

The yellow snake will protect me
and be my messenger.
She will take my prayer quickly
to the gods of the western mountains.
May it be happy in front of me.

In the early light
saguaros climb single file
to meet me.
Each carries birds' nests and flowers
and each holds securely
in his huge fists
the fragile life lines
of tiny spiders who ride the wind.
May it be happy on either side of me.

I walk with a god behind me.
I walk with a god in front of me.
I walk with a god on either side of me.

16

The mountain which moves is holy.
As it turns around
it draws all things to it.
It draws the clouds and birds.
They circle around it.
Soon the rain hides it.

A handsome man comes out of the rain
wearing a necklace of white shells.
The light from his necklace
flashes over the world.
His eyes are black as the rain cloud.
His teeth are white as shells.
He is silent and draws the clouds to him.

In one hand he carries a branch
of dark spruce. With the other
he sprinkles pollen before him
over the wet ground.

17

I go to the Woman Who Changes.
Her sister leads me
with a white shell in her hand.

In the evening it will rain.
All night it will rain.
In the morning I will smell wild onions.

My song is short because I know so much.

From

The Tattooed Desert

1971

The Past

mask I have worn and discarded
staring with blind eyes at the mountains
how does it feel to be there
when the light arrives to meet you

HISTORY

always on the horizon someone
is holding up a red thing
like a butchered cow its eyes
are as distant as old photographs

we invent the past we give it
to anyone who happens along it is
a bottomless lake with only
one shore and near it
we build our contradictions
towers with both clocks and bells
steps leading up to a blind wall

I do not understand war or history

the signs read *this way out*
it is a long way and there were
so many people I loved so many
people I could have loved

HE WHO REMAINS

you have so much to give they said
so I gave it now it is gone

I stand with my back to a cliff
where stones lean over
looking down at me they are smooth
they have dragged themselves
a long way to get here

years ago I wrote love letters
to distant water and wore
the desire to travel like a hair shirt

but that is over and regret
was never a friend of mine so I
let him go in search of the others
who departed wearing accidental lives
mocking me calling me *he who remains*

and I remain in the desert
caught in the ropes of myself
like rosaries staying here with penitent
stars whose confessions frighten me

there is no explanation for lights
which move about inside the mountains
and coyotes are all that is left
of a race we once conquered

at night I hear them worshiping
gods with unspeakable names

I have learned to make use of pain
he never fails to take me
into his confidence telling me
more than I wanted to know

and when morning arrives bringing
whatever it can to help I ready myself
for the impetuous revival of sand

if I were to leave this desert
who would cherish transparent
light who would nurse broken stones
who would mother the cold

LETTER FROM AN INLAND PROVINCE

late in the afternoon
when the light walks up and leans against me
I stand there like nobody I ever heard of
I just stand there

the poets have gone in search of words
and the prophets stayed home to wait
but I am a depot to which the trains
stopped coming years ago

once I saw long rubbery arms
torn up from the sea like snakes
I heard what the sand was saying
I listened all night while a monocle
chattered to the moon on the water
it was madness a kind of magnificence

I still know the words but I forget to pray them
it has never been easy
fighting the desire to eat glass

NEW YEAR'S EVE

The year is boarding
a clipper ship with frozen sails.
Soon it will depart through the terrible
refraction of water, carrying
dust in its mouth.

It had nothing particular
to recommend it, no Halley's comet, no
quintuplets, no two-headed calf.
It leaves no watermark on the wallpaper.
Yet it was sweet, it was sweet to us.

It was built from the raw
materials of small disasters and a summer
when the birds ate all the peaches.
We feel as if we have been telling
stories to which no one listened.

And it leaves behind a display case
from which each of us chooses
his own hands. The hands fit us
like gloves and we slip them on.
We stand on the dock
clutching our dead gods
and old poets while the ship
lingers like the afterbirth
of sound, the silent bombast
at the terminal of memory.

VALEDICTION

I who witnessed the nail's desire
for a blind hammer
and kept account books of rain

have got through the day without hope
what an accomplishment
now I can drop my eyes like stones
into the black water of night

I am taking myself apart
like a puzzle

this must be an ear this must be
a piece of my coat
or is it sky which there is so much of
and all the same color

I am resigning from my shoes
they are worn out
and will fit anybody

whoever wears them
his job will be to harvest
the wrinkled shells of walnuts

he must remember the signals
how to speak to ducks
about their carelessness
how to remind trees they have
a certain responsibility

he must prevent the sleepy road
from stumbling into the river
and watch for tiny fish
who swim past
carrying great burdens of light

APRIL

returns like an expatriate, a defector
from the frost. Her feet are wrapped
in old rose petals, her eyes
are the color of wet sand under moss.

She guides a wounded caravan
of spiders and dilapidated memories.
Combing her dripping hair with elegant
fingers, she announces the forsythia and pain.

She waits in the summerhouse
for summer while the moon comes in empty,
a ship bearing her transparent name.

STRANGERS

we find ourselves at the exact place
where the light becomes darkness
and turn our faces toward one another

realizing we could be lovers we could
be anything we could even be friends
we could carry our scars
like banners we could pray to each other
and answer each other's prayers

with so much need on the horizon
surely there is a heart around here somewhere
but we are characters from a book who have
come here on vacation
to listen to the pulse of the sea
which makes an affirmation beyond despair

those who have heard it
do not recommend it to anybody

we have heard the hypnotized telephone
ring itself into a trance of silence we have
seen the poor pass by on borrowed legs
we have been enameled by the sun

day lingers on the undersides of leaves
and as we are slowly going
under water where all light
is the light of a green stone broken open
we keep our distance it is all we have

SATURDAY NIGHT AT THE ELK'S CLUB

Entering, I find friends everywhere.
Those who can afford to be gracious
lift their glasses to those who cannot
afford to pay for the drinks. We
are all brothers here. We tell
prophetic lies and wait.

A girl comes in. She is nobody's
daughter. She is like a virgin
wearing petals of the flowering peach.
When she lies down it is
for a purpose and when she rises
it is for her pay. She says
For love this time, only for love.
Nobody believes her.

The door is locked. Someone
gets up to make a speech.
He says *For love this time, only
for love.* Several of us have our guns
ready but I shoot him. They hold
me down and pound my face
until morning arrives dragging Sunday
behind it like a tired slave.
We are all brothers here.

THE WHITE HOTEL

For John Weston

when winter comes
adjust your voice to it
when the clock dies hide it
from the children

do not resist the urge to travel
it will be only a journey
and there is no arrival

but drive through the desert quickly
it is inhabited by those
in search of death

beside a gabardine sea you will find
the white hotel where bougainvillea
drips from the roof like blood

dim lights will be on in the hallway
a long moss carpet
flowing past a wilderness of doors
stairs crowded with unpredictable
lovers and assassins

in the bar new arrivals
celebrate reunions by throwing
their glasses into the fireplace
others just drop them on the floor

when anything falls down
in this hotel it lies there forever

all night they will sing old songs
when the shoe tree blooms
in the desert
and the ice plant melts by the sea
all night the water will rest
quietly in its blue tomb

at dawn when palm trees
wave their arms as they do at the slightest
change in plans you will watch
the waves send up
fine contingents of water
each retreating without losing its courage
thousands of white truces
negotiated on the sand

and with your pulse beating for distance
your hair turning to salt
you will walk into the water
and say *because of its great depth*
the sea can forgive anything

but do not linger
at the white hotel or soon you will learn
that memory is the only
kind of loss we ever know

CONNAIS-TU LE PAYS?

I have discovered a country
where the pages of books are all
margins and the calendar is frozen
in a wall of ice. Its mirrors are kept
in cages and covered at night.

I cross its border by way
of the labyrinth in the radiator.
The doors close behind me.

The guards at the gate of the principal
city are dangerous. Also
the porter who hangs on the wall
like a silver knife. As for the troll
who once lured me under a bridge,
I blame him for everything.

There is no map of the city
but I know my way.
When I get to my room
the others are waiting: the child
with tiny blue fish in her hair,
the ghost with a flashlight,
the prince who died of a bloody
nose and the angel who guards him,
the white nun dragging
her long black shadow.

I show them the sand I have
smuggled in my shoes, and my letters
written on dry grass.
I bring them a yellow wax
flower in a green pot.
We celebrate the silence.

At night when it rains we paint
a small fire on the wall
and sit before it, drinking
from cups made of buttons.
We drink to the present which is
eternal. We drink to the delicate
shells which grow in the garden,
to salt rising up
from the earth like smoke,
to another safe journey.

Outside, the water is moving
past in search of some
low place to lie down.

AUGUST

All summer
surrounded by unconditioned air
my father has been dying.

Anybody coming by here at night
could see me looking out the open window
and wonder what I am waiting for:

the stars to move perhaps,
the big dipper on its delicate
hinges to tilt,
the earth to cool.

Today smelled like burning rope
and tonight the moon is cut in half.
Promises are unimportant to us now.
The past is sufficient.

I choose his memories with care
and hold them before vague eyes
as if they were charms on a string.

Life drops from his white hand,
a scarab falling into thick grass,
and the look on the face of silence
is surprise.

NOVEMBER

1

when I arrived
stone crosses hung from the eaves
and ambulances were lined up at the door
like hungry mice

the wound I left here years ago
I asked them
has it healed yet

your father is sleeping they told me
come back tomorrow we are
closed for the night

but just at that moment
out of breath and wearing
somebody else's clothes
a funeral rushed into the hospital
barely in time to rescue the dead

2

before that I was saying
something different I was
a flag trying to escape from its pole

now I enumerate the qualities of silence
first the stars which are pores
in the skin of night then my birth
which did not include me
then each leaf falling
as one wing flying away
without its mate

3

my father went in search of death
like a mole
blind and beautiful

all summer he listened
to the inner voice of his pain
rising in a song clear and high
dragging the music after it

his life was an unmade bed
nobody rich or famous ever slept there

he put his face into the fire
and said *I will not keep you waiting*

4

wherever the rain goes tonight
I will go with it
through the city I was born in
city of monuments the statues their
lethargy their cold wet faces

the names of the streets
are climbing into the mountains
and the mountains are holding their names
up to a dark sky

weeping birches continue to weep
for us and for each other
I cannot comfort them

I carry myself slowly
past the houses of the important where
they live among their habits
as comfortably as water on stone
the doors are asleep
in the arms of their hinges
I leave them sleeping

at every step
darkness seeps from the holes in my shoes
I am cold as an empty glove

from the sidewalk
I pick up a black walnut
locked in its shriveled skin like a mummy
Father I say to it tenderly
old Father it was harder than hell
to love you
and impossible not to

look what November has done to us both

SURGERY

you watched them at work
with their knives and scissors

you watched them sewing you up
hope with his needle and thread
attacking the helpless eyes of your buttons

knowing that all you really needed of yourself
was the part they would not let you keep

CORTEGE

inside a lung somewhere
a star is falling

the widow
is what is left over
she will get used to it

in the meantime
the mourners have been paid
and dismissed they can
go home we can
all go home

where the tongue
we left on the windowsill
to ripen in silence
is beginning to wake up
and speak
the exact words of the dead

REUNION

once a year at midnight
the ghost of my father walks in
wearing his scars
on the outside of his bandages
asking directions *which
way are we going
how far to silence*

maps flapping on the walls
the walls falling in and me
waiting as usual while the future
limps from door to door
on its broken toes

sliding into a chair
and tucking one leg under him
he lets his head begin
to fall toward his right
shoulder as he gives me a long

wink and says *I'm going
to get drunk again tonight
god how I dread it*

THE CROSSING

The journey is always return.
What I cannot leave behind I take
with me: my hands like dry vines
torn from a wall, the memory
of strangers, the smell of wet sidewalks
worn into the soles of my shoes.

Just after dawn the river exposes
its wound and I cross a bridge
in love with its own reflection.
A few lights are still on in houses
downriver. A rowboat half sunk
in the mud is calling for help.
Even from this distance I can tell
the trees are crippled with age.

I am full of other places and tired
like birds who return in the spring.
I stumble through jonquils the color
of flesh, past holy places
where lovers and children have made
nests in the matted grass.

They are flying flags in the city
of flags, so many at half mast,
so many in my honor. They keep up
appearances. I enter the city
through a gate as old as smoke
and have returned to my own people.

Those beside whom this river
passes always, will they forgive me
the distance? Those without eyes
who count days by fingering notches
on sticks, those who grow thin
in silence, who do not permit
their clothes to touch their bodies,
who have only their names to guide them.

I walk among them. They bow
two by two, with their arms
around one another. The signs
say *Keep Moving*, the flowers are stone
faces covered with moss. I had
no idea the dead lived so well.

THE TATTOOED DESERT

at whatever page the book fell open
I read it
and knelt beside every bed

they could have baptized me
in any tub and fitted me with secondhand
wings at the auction
I wouldn't have minded

but the gods turned out to be
grotesques they paraded before me
as if for inspection with dirty gauze
over their eyes
when the road forked they took
both ways they disguised themselves
as places I couldn't find
their feathers turned into ferns and when I
reached out to them
they were distant landscapes
moving through my fingers and leaving
a strange smell on my hands

while the old hat under the tower was telling
the same story and a toothless mouth
was getting ready to grin
the one with a face like a pig
began to eat his own fingers
and I ran away

they initialed the space I left
empty but they found me again
upstairs in the back bedroom of another house
with whisky hitting my tongue
like a hammer
and again I climbed out the window and slid
down a tree in the gothic rain

I must have been almost crazy
to start out alone like that on my bicycle
pedaling into the tropics carrying
a medicine for which no one had found
the disease and hoping
I would make it in time

I passed through a paper village under glass
where explorers first found
silence and taught it to speak
where old men were sitting in front
of their houses killing sand without mercy

brothers I shouted to them
tell me who moved the river
where can I find a good place to drown

slowly they raised their heads
this is the tattooed desert they told me
all that will survive of it will be
what you remember
then they went into their flaming
houses and closed the doors

and I rode on through the disappointed night
with my pulse beating like a ticket
about to be torn while the mountains
tried every possible position and finally
slept with their backs to one another

when I found the river it was
what I expected just an old wall lying down
covered with pictures

dead mystics were buried on its banks
each with his telephone beside him I recognized
the place I knew all the secret
passages it must have been
where I was born

the gentle eyes of the river
looked up without reproach and those
floating past spoke to me
this is cremation by water they said *we who are
burned here rise up without ashes
we are repeated
in the sound of wax bells ringing
and the testimony of mouthless trees*

while they spoke the sky arrived
and I saw the perfect complexion of light
the wind was blowing the mountains away
at an incredible speed and suddenly
it was the morning after nothing

my faithful servant Pain
who had followed me all this way
approached holding out a gift and I took it
a sleeping bat gorged with blood

all day I will carry it with me
as a reminder to those who try to take me back
see I will say
holding it up to them
we have survived another night

GAMBIT

I have boarded up the stations of waiting
where mice buy tickets to nowhere
and windows listen for announcements
of broken glass. Let the hands
of dead clocks rest
on the final numbers of chance.
The distance is over.

I have discarded the menu for lunch
and the menu for dinner. Each day
I choose something different to forget
and clear light arrives, bringing
the sea as it should be, the boats
where they are. I go forward
while irreplaceable leaves drip
from green cages and spiders
are playing their webs like guitars.

In one hand I carry your picture
to guide me and with the other
I am combing your name through my hair.

From

Of All the Dirty Words

1972

We the People

in the distance
some band is playing

a march
which started out as a waltz
and got carried away

and we are marching

THE SOLDIERS RETURNING

it was almost easy to say goodby
we said it we kept saying it *goodby*
goodby no one was listening

we traveled
pretending we were pursued by something good
in spite of empty horizons

we stood on the parapets of distant hunger
and slept in strange beds
in the red-light districts of the impotent

sometimes we knew
what we were doing and did it
sometimes we were not sure

now we return as the white hand
returns to its glove
and how to convince the darkness we are here
when it has so many others to care for

we return bearing the secret
that there is no secret
no collusion no plot
wars occur because men want them
and peace occurs when they are tired

we who were hired to kill
but not by anyone we could name
not by anyone we could talk to about it
return to the terrible menace of love
and to our children

WAR

each day the terror wagon
passes while elevators
hesitate between floors
and frightened windows
cover their eyes

the bell rings *bring out*
your dead bring out your dead
the bell keeps ringing

we are sad quiet men
in a difficult century

we run our treacherous
fingers through their hair
one last time
and trade our children
for the most expensive
versions of old lies

WHY I NEVER WENT INTO POLITICS

For Brad

my son
I promised you a world and see
it is all gone it is beyond
repairing we must learn
to live without it

each day a parade of soldiers
goes past followed by dogs
whose clinking tags proclaim
they have owners
and they are not mad

we are told not to look up or down
the sky is not public the earth
is not ours
we are told to look
straight ahead and march forward
and kill
that is the way it is done
in this land

my son
I love you and having told you
all I remember all that is left
of an old story
I tell you that those
who use the language of poets
are poets and those
who use the language of thieves
are thieves

THE HEROES OF OUR TIME

are so thin they can stand
in the rain without getting wet

when they walk on the beach
they see each wave
leaping over the bones of its father
and as the bones melt they see
beneath them the teeth
still smiling

the heroes of our time
know the intimate gestures of trees

when the wind approaches them
rings grow on their fingers
carnelian amethyst topaz

when they speak and when they listen
it is always with their hands

when they fold their arms
they express a great silence
and we who complained
of the promiscuity of lightning
begin to experiment with flints

the heroes of our time
are clarity surrounded with darkness
need in the absence of prayer

light runs through their veins
and returns with the answers
to their questions

when they die
their names are buried
under hidden monuments but their
bodies are scattered on battlefields
and soon wheat grows again
in the ruined fields

the wheat bows to the wheat
and is harvested and a few grains
are left on the ground
to be gathered
by the heroes of our time

SEVEN PRELUDES TO SILENCE

1

All day a wounded mountain followed me,
gentle and crumpled like a fern.
It was too shy to speak of its great need
and what could I have done to help it?

2

The desert has forgotten what it is waiting for.
Even sand will not survive without a purpose.
Can dust learn to swim? Will flowers
be able to repeat themselves in stone?

3

We have removed the earth's flesh and torn out
its bleeding veins. Sunlight reflects
from our knives. It blisters the surface
of the lake where nebulae of fish will never
return. A few gulls carry their white grief
on delicate hollow bones from water to water.

4

We have forgotten that once there were black
swans with brilliant red beaks and curly
tail feathers. Soon the last birds of desperate
passage will ricochet through our oily rooms.

5

The stars confirm nothing, deny nothing. Heads
of animals grow on our walls. Their hopeless
glass eyes stare down at us without reproach.

6

We who invented the clock and the metronome
cannot keep the calendar alive. We exist,
not on the edge of life but at its limits,
asking no pardon of the grass or the empty
shells which arrive and depart on each tide.

7

In the book of our history it will be recorded
that we murdered the earth. With the name
of a different crime tattooed on each finger
we walk out into the orchard and find
tiny mirrors hanging from the trees. Listen.
The leaves are breaking as they fall.

WINTER

his gloves were meant
for better hands
his hands for better gloves

the story of his life
gets smaller and disappears

when spring arrives
who will support the cause of snow
hanging like a sound from a trumpet
frozen in the distance

and how can water live that way
without asking permission of anybody
a quiet voice with a short memory

who can it love
attracting light
and the moss beneath it
as soft as a snail's foot

the eyes of the stones
even if they cannot see will listen
with all the senses of their colors

and ghosts of sycamores
will wait for darkness
when they can embrace each other
like smoke

but winter has looked
into so many houses

he knows that when you are poor
nothing is ever enough
and when you are rich it is the same

BROTHER

you still carry
your guilt around for company
I will not deprive you of it
but I have an empty space
where my hate lived
while I nursed it
as if it were a child

brother my only
brother it was too late for us
before we were born

it was too late
before you learned to be brutal
and I learned to be weak

your childhood
was a hallway of doors
each closing just as you
got to it
but I was younger
and all the doors were closed
before I could walk

how could I have expected you
to save me when you could
not save yourself

brother my only
brother if not from you
from whom did I learn
so much despair

I went in search
of a father and found you
with a whip in your hand
but what were you searching for
in such dark places
where I was searching for love

55

THE OTHER WORLD

I can tell you this much
without incriminating anyone:
There is another world.
In that world the dust
pleads for attention
and the bones of one skeleton
are always tangled
among the bones of another.

The eyes of those who live there
are as blind and fragile
as eggshells. Pain is visible
in the twisted fingers of their hair.
Nothing is repairable.

There is a lighthouse in the desert
with black gulls wheeling around it
screaming for rain.
Tall minarets of fire
rise from withered sand.
We build bridges to attract
a river but none comes.

By day there are academies of silence.
At night we hear the hungry
bleating of carnivorous lambs.

If I told you the truth
about everyone who lives there
you would believe me. You would
cry a long time
but you would believe me.
You would never be the same again.

LETTER TO A LOST FRIEND

War, trade, religious debts to discharge, these are mostly the reasons for men's distant journeyings: but you take pleasure in distant journeys without reason. —St.-John Perse

we do not realize what we want
until we learn
what we are willing to give up for it
and you did God knows you did

when swimming was no longer possible
you learned to sink you learned
to live at the bottom of the sea

now tell me of the chambers where you sleep
tell me it does not matter
lie if you must

is your bed luminous is it festooned
with seaweed do all your narrow windows
open onto water
is the tide kind to you

forgive me if I do not understand

last night a stranger asked me *what
gives you most pleasure* and before I thought
I answered her *revenge*

THE RAIN THE STONES THE DARKNESS

my father died
having given the matter much thought and decided
having first released me from the commandment
having become the child he knew I needed and I carried him in my arms
leaving me his childhood because mine had been taken from me by others
showing me the proper way to die because I did not know how

my father died
surrounded by those who loved him and they were few
surrounded by those he loved and they were fewer
leaving no division among us for there was nothing to divide
and the earth which we had already divided unequally accepted him who had no part in that division

my father died
and the neighbors went on fighting but the rain which was to come would calm them
and the tools he handled went on living in the hands of those less competent
and no sympathy was called for so none came

my father died
leaving the question of darkness to the darkness and the question of light to the light
and the pain which had lived in his house had nowhere to go
so it died with him and was buried barefoot
because he had not worn shoes in a long time

my father died
having arrived too late having arrived too early
having been absent most of his life and otherwise at the wrong place

my father died
the night the saints rise from their graves and he passed them moving in the opposite direction
holding one hand out to the window and saying words I could not translate
having already told me all I would need to know
but would not remember until later

my father died
before rain came but he knew it was coming
and the rain which had been waiting fell on us to make it easier
and dust settled on the eyes of the water but the water did not close its eyes
and hoops fell from the barrels and rust arrived to take possession of its country
and all his lives died and some are easier to forget than others

my father died
in bed and sober who would have preferred to die drunk and on his feet in a bar
and those who had known him as someone else
remembered him in places I had never been
and took nothing from me and would have given me all they remembered if they could

my father died
having received what he had waited for
and whatever it was I gave it to him
and we both knew he would take it with him
and it would never be a burden to anyone else again

my father died
poor and the mourners came and went away quickly
but all night the stones were opulent with rain

HER

her hair burns and is never consumed
her eyebrows are infinite
her eyelids are blue clouds
over blue mountains at dawn
her eyes know separate worlds
yet both speak the same language

her nostrils divide a kingdom between them
her lips are beaches on whose sand I sleep
her teeth are tiny fingers
her tongue is silence
at the mention of her silence I listen

her ears are mornings which hold
the secrets of afternoons in their arms
her temples are pools of water in a mirage
her chin is a pear I take in my mouth
her neck holds bruises as if they were born there
her breasts are twins
one remembers what the other forgets

her arms are light reflected on water
her hands are braided milk
her fingers are keys to the locks of my body
her fingernails are moons rising in wax
her thighs are a nest of dark pearls
seeing in all directions

her legs rise up early to surround me
her knees are stirrups for my shoulders
her ankles know the truth and repeat it
her feet walk on air as if it were water
her odor is the odor of the young syringa

inside her is a secret place
where a star about to explode is waiting

MY LOVE

when the crows fly away
with their compassion
and I remain to eat
whatever is left of my heart

I think of my love
with the odor of salt
of my love who holds me in her eyes
as if I were whole and beautiful

and I think of those
who walk the streets all night
frantic with desire and bruised
by the terrible small lips of rain

I touch you
as a blind man touches the dice
and finds he has won

FOR LOIS

love
it takes so long
to learn who we are
then it is always the wrong one

I am growing old
and no one comes to my rescue

the weak are spectators
the powerful are somewhere else
managing their own desires

I am so tired
dull scissors could finish my story

love
if I could only
be sure about the future
I would sleep a little while
or be dead a little while
and wake to find you

THE FOURTEENTH ANNIVERSARY

And Jacob served seven years for Rachel;
and they seemed unto him but a few days,
for the love he had to her.

—*Genesis 29:20*

1

in winter when each day is harvested
we come out of darkness into the light
of a fire built from what is left over

with our decisions postponed
and our shadows no longer wearing
their daytime shoes

it is as if we have something to say
to the fire but we keep forgetting

later when you are asleep
I walk through these rooms
adjusting my mask to the silence

the fire is dying and outside
the moon is a knock waiting with no door

2

we came out of childhood into a room
with all its vases waiting for flowers
into a luxury of absent flowers
and the light was different

how easily the moon insinuates herself
among the clouds how shyly she undresses
and how quickly she reclines

with my hands reaching
to lock the door which was opening
in the moment it was opening I noticed
the simplicities
I had removed from my pockets
and left on a table by the wrong bed
for anyone to see

these things have never been resolved
will never be resolved

3

do not believe what they say about me
it is true but it is not the truth

the truth is hidden
in the brain of a green bird who cannot sing
the truth is in one seed of a pomegranate
among thousands of pomegranates

the truth is on the moon's white lips
as she sinks into the sea
strange silent lady
worshiped by men who lie in the mud
beneath her slender foot

4

finding they cannot walk on water
some men sink while others
go into the desert and never return

the sea is willing the sea accepts everything
but those who walk in the desert
travel in circles and arrive
always at the same place
with dawn close behind them
trailing frail light as if it were hair

walking in the desert
I have begun to see into my body's rivers
whose banks are ivory and pearl
with bridges of muscle stretching above them
pulsing in time to the music of the nerves

inside the bones the light
is failing but I see small things
crawling over the floor on urgent business
like beetles on strings

I see into my sex and it is not
a jewel it is a small fire
tended by old men who are dying

a small fire in a great dark house
where the wind comes through the walls
and a book turns its own pages carefully
so as not to miss anything

I read in the book that all the glory
of the kings I have not known
and all the beauty of the queens
will die when that fire dies

5

then I take my tongue to your body
letting it wander blind over your ribs
as if each were one string of a harp
leaving no string untouched

we reach our hands deep into one another
and if they come up at all
they come up full of poetry the moon
a few stars and a silence rinsed in blood

who dares speak against that silence
let him speak

I have loved you honestly
with all my crooked heart and gently
as darkness comes to water
and in passion with the storm

of all the nothings I have ever said
one word remains
I wear it as a wafer on my tongue
it is your name

6

bind up the sagging breasts of morning
oh my darling let the light in

your hair is more beautiful than dawn

we have arrived years later
at the starting place
now we shall begin again

DESERT WATER

once a year
when infallible toads
begin to sing
all the spiders who left me
return and I make room for them

I am too proud
to mention their long absence

then the owls
send a message in code
from saguaro to saguaro
and the toads stop singing

a sea of warm air
rolls over quickly and relaxes
we wait for the promised rain
for the second coming
of water

each time it arrives
like the flood and I know
I have not wasted my life

spiders still come
to my house for shelter

SAN JUAN'S DAY

during summer in these latitudes
one disappointment is as good as another

each year when the rains come
we are convinced by the sophistries of water
that the dust will not be back

and each year it returns unerringly
falling upon us
like the patience we have forgotten we possess

CHOOSE ONE FROM AMONG THEM

1

the whore has her knowledge
of man beyond rescue

to be held by many men in one night
knowing that not one of them
will hold anyone else that night

whether it is better to spend a life
not knowing what you want
or to spend a life knowing
exactly what you want
and that you will never have it

one of my hands was born in this kingdom
and one in the other

2

beauty cannot be looked at steadily
for very long
yet it is impossible to change one's voice
without changing one's life

how many times have I tried unsuccessfully
to forget what it was like to be a child

and do not condemn the liar for his lie
perhaps he was created to tell that lie
and we were created to listen
believe or not believe
as it was appointed

3

the forms of love are myriad as stars
and some men fall through space
for a lifetime
without touching any of them

love letters written in lemon juice
menus written in blood
the world is ruined no doubt
but even its bones are beautiful

and we are the guests of the slaughter
with words smeared on our lips like grease

when we have used up all the words
we will find the silences waiting for us
and choose one from among them

4

when I am in a room it is not empty
I am old enough to sing
cry dance or laugh without company
I can even sleep alone

the essential thing
is not that I have chosen to be a prisoner
but that I have chosen
what to be a prisoner of

and it was so simple
now that it is accomplished I forget
I ever made the choice

to live in the desert
this place which permits me to remain
where I have learned to call spiders
by their first names
little brothers of my darkness

where silence is nourishment
and each ghost carries
the ghost of tomorrow in his arms

where dawn arrives like fire
and every morning I am here to meet it
waiting to follow its instructions

REQUIEM FOR SONORA

1

a small child of a wind
stumbles toward me down the arroyo
lost and carrying no light
tearing its sleeves
on thorns of the palo verde
talking to itself
and to the dark shapes it touches
searching for what it has not lost
and will never find
searching
and lonelier
than even I can imagine

the moon sleeps
with her head on the buttocks of a young hill
and you lie before me
under moonlight as if under water
oh my desert
the coolness of your face

2

men are coming inland to you
soon they will make you the last resort
for tourists who have
nowhere else to go

what will become of the coyote
with eyes of topaz
moving silently to his undoing
the ocotillo
flagellant of the wind
the deer climbing with dignity
further into the mountains
the huge and delicate saguaro

what will become of those who cannot learn
the terrible knowledge of cities

3

years ago I came to you as a stranger
and have never been worthy
to be called your lover or to speak your name
loveliest
most silent sanctuary
more fragile than forests
more beautiful than water

I am older and uglier
and full of the knowledge
that I do not belong to beauty
and beauty does not belong to me
I have learned to accept
whatever men choose to give me
or whatever they choose to withhold
but oh my desert
yours is the only death I cannot bear

CODA

be private
let no one but strangers touch you

go out in madness
and observe the lidless eye of the moon

return in madness
wear madness under your skin

compress failure into a stone
compress the stone into a jewel

crush the jewel into dust
and eat the dust

learn to feed and water silence
be merciful to trees which shelter you

kneel at the feet of mountains
guard the desert while it sleeps

From

Chosen Place

1975

Outcast

I was raised in a state of mind
where those who know nothing
are sure about everything.
I migrated, with difficulty,
into a state of indecision,
but I will never be forgiven
by those I left behind.

DREAM OF RETURN

Through the window I can see them.
They are eating. The silver
reflects light from the chandelier.
There is a fire in the fireplace.

I stand outside knocking, but they
will not open the door. I tell them
I am cold and need shelter, promising
to ask for no food, to lean
against nothing. I will leave my dogs
outside, even my luggage, and will stay
only one night. I will be gone
early in the morning. I am very quiet.
They will not even know I am there.

When they open the door, I rush in
without wiping my feet, shouting
for wine like a maniac and bringing
everything with me. I have come home.

AFTER THIRTY YEARS

I still remember Ed and Clyde,
the house painter and the paperhanger,
who left their families in middle age
to share one mistress in a bottle. When I
was a child they were inseparable, a pair
of cards, the Ace and King of Alcohol.

Clyde had an ancient panel truck.
Ed couldn't drive and had no license.
One night as they started down a hill
Clyde dozed at the wheel and fell clear out.
Two blocks later the cops found Ed,
drunk as a lord, alone in the cab
of a panel truck which had hit three cars.
Clyde hid. Ed did some time behind bars.
Clyde came to see him every day. Ed never told.

Years later, Ed told Clyde what we all knew:
Clyde's daughter was a whore. Clyde swung
on Ed, and swore. They never spoke again.
Clyde died first. In a hospital. Bad liver.
Ed died in a gutter with his ribs kicked in,
nobody knew what for. His son became a lawyer
and a judge. Clyde's daughter just paid off
her daddy's debts and stayed a whore.

NOTES TOWARD AN AUTOBIOGRAPHY

don't expect smiles on all my faces
you won't have to look close
to see what I am
or what I want to become
or that I'm not becoming it

if you see me from a certain angle
on a better than average day
you will notice I am the other one
not the one you expected

it will appear that I have chosen
my shadow for its good behavior
and that I am bored by those women
whose bodies are all
they have to say to me

I will seduce
neither your wife nor your son
but I must tell you
that inside every thin poet
is a fat poet trying to get out

I do my best to keep him prisoner
don't offer me a second helping
of anything

———◆•••◆———

when I remember where I came from
and how much I owe my sources
it is difficult to continue

I see my life flapping over the ground
the shadow of a dark wing
with no bird to guide it

but this too is self-indulgence
like guilt

it would be better to say
I will do what I can to entertain you
and for what I lack the courage to do
please forgive me

I would prefer to be completely honest
but then you would hate me
you see of course that we all
lie for the same reasons

the hungry bat
in search of a vein is shameless
but more honest than any of us
can afford to be

———◆•••▶———

living in the desert
has taught me to go inside myself
for shade

———◆•••▶———

I am capable of giving rich gifts
when they are unexpected
but when someone asks me
for a match
I blush and fumble
embarrassed to give so much upon demand

———◆•••▶———

I have a good marriage

a good marriage
is how we resolve the conflict
between who we want to go to bed with
and whose bed we want to wake up in

it's always a compromise

———◆••◆———

my old poems come back as strangers
and gradually I recognize
a gesture a worn-out coat
a tired smile

these were my companions
when I had no one else and they
were kind to me

how could I deny them now
when others speak only of their faults

———◆••◆———

showing the desert to visitors
makes it real to me

when I say *this is an arroyo*
this is a palo verde this is a saguaro
these things exist
as if to support what I am saying
and the visitors believe me

but after they go back
to wherever they came from
and I walk through the desert alone
I know the truth about this landscape

it does not exist
I dreamed it

————◆◆◆◆►————

the inevitable consequence
of a well-directed life is death
and the inevitable consequence
of a misdirected life
is also death

at night I keep telling myself
go to sleep nobody is to blame
we are what we are
the world is what it is

and eventually I go to sleep
but I never believe it

THE BOTTOM LINE

For William Stafford

You and I think about it: who pays
the price for the way we live?
Some people live so still
they incur no expenses. Others,
so wild there's the Devil to pay.
Some don't even know they're in debt
and others go slow to avoid it.

People like you pay as you go
and people like me live in debt,
but we know who we owe. I owe
a woman, a good woman, and I
will never be able to pay.

People like you are beautiful
and free of all debt. The best
that can be said for people like me
is that we know who we owe.

You Can't Have Everything

1975

The Future

bright bird with one wing
flying in circles over the place
where morning gets up
stiff from having slept
all night on the damp ground

tomorrow has already happened
how fortunate we are
that we can't remember it

THE POET OF SANTO TOMAS

If you live where I come from
and you want to be rich and beautiful,
first get rich.
Then we'll tell you
you're beautiful.
Hell! Settle for that.
You can't have everything.

Walk down Main Street at midnight
when the only places open
are two bars in the same block.
Turn the corner and walk past the homes
of the good people of Santo Tomas.
Everybody will be doing
one of three things, rather well:
sleeping, drinking, or the thing
we all think we would do better
with somebody else's husband or wife.
And maybe a guardian angel,
like a huge white moth,
will be hovering over each of us.

Years ago some desperate farmers
took this land away from the desert,
and every summer
the desert tries to get it back.
In the heat everything stops moving,
even the dogs. All night
cicadas drill our teeth.
Water gets scarce
and what little there is
is warm and bitter, but we learn
to drink our liquor straight.

New people come here
sometimes, but don't stay long.
I'd like to know what attracts them.
Maybe the need to suffer,
we all have it
like a bird pecking away inside us
as if inside an egg.
Some people think
that if you suffer enough
you get to be better, even noble;
but I've lived here forty years
and I get meaner every day.

I have nothing to recommend me
except longevity. And hell,
what good is that?
Show me an old man who doesn't envy
every young stud he sees
and I'll show you a body
with the undertaker's fingerprints
all over it.

Because of the way they dress
it's getting hard to tell the whores
from the female schoolteachers,
which probably means that whoring
isn't as well paid a profession
as it used to be,
what with all the enthusiastic amateurs
around here lately.

I used to think this bar
was the center of the community
and if I sat here long enough
I'd learn everything worth knowing
about the good people of Santo Tomas.
But this afternoon I went to the funeral
of the richest man in town
and watched his widows,
the old one and the young one,
fighting over which of them
would walk behind his coffin to the grave.
Now I realize
that all significant social events
still take place in church.

The earth is moving several ways at once
but sometimes I wonder
if we are going with it.
And when the drive-in movie
shuts down for the night,
the stars remain over Santo Tomas
like holes in the darkness
through which we see a cold, enormous light.

I don't think death will be much use to us
since we've grown accustomed
to using pain for our purposes,
and even love when we have to.
I think death will arrive
when we have nothing left to use
to get what we want
or when we no longer want anything,
whichever comes first.

I've learned to wait.
Nothing we ever want
is worth what we go through to get it,
and the difference between
what little we have to offer
and how much we're asked to pay
is life, a kind of debt
we always owe somebody.
I'm in no hurry to pay it.

If you can't make it in Newark
milking the canaries,
you can leave your wedding cake
and go to Cleveland
or Des Moines or Little Rock.

If you can't make it there
because of the humidity,
you can go to Tucson
to drink the air and live in the sun.
If you can't make it in Tucson
because of the heat,
you can go to California
and wear dark glasses.

And if you can't make it in California,
you can go to Hell, it isn't far.
The border runs
right through Los Angeles.

THE SEVEN AGES OF MAN

1. The Age of Miracles

returns to a small
village in Peru

they recognize him
at once and rush out
to meet him singing

carrying cripples
and diseased children

after the ceremony
they are happier
than they have ever been

they proclaim a holiday
of joy and divide

his flesh among them
placing his bones
carefully like seeds

in a new grave

2. The Age of Romance

sits on a hill
and looks toward the sea

beyond him the surface
of the water tears light
into thousands of pieces

and throws them
in all directions

soon he will get up
and return to his house
in the city

91

he will look out the window
and it will be twilight

darkness will begin to build
its nest under the eaves
this beautiful pain

lasts such a short time
he will say

and so few notice it

3. The Age of Desire
walks all night through streets
of a foreign city whose language
he does not speak

his feet are delicate
his boots highly polished

in each lighted window
he sees images of what his life
could be if it were real

he knows exactly what he wants
but cannot find it

every morning he returns
to his small ugly room
takes out a loaded revolver

places it on the table
and writes in his diary

the entry for tomorrow

4. The Age of Despair

rides into town
on a crippled horse

his eyes are pale and blue
his eyebrows droop
like twin mustaches

his worn suitcase
is covered with labels

Bombay Marrakesh Rome
Brisbane Tampico Des Moines
Fairbanks La Tierra Eterna

he looks at the muddy
streets and wooden sidewalks

his eyes shift
toward the mountains
he knows this place

is like all the others

5. The Age of War

poses like a young man
on his wedding night

his magnificent profile
appears on the coins
of many countries

beneath the mask
his eye sockets are empty

he is older than anyone
but our hearts cannot resist
a man so young and beautiful

and so blind

6. The Age of Elegance

arrives and there is
no one to meet him
no porters no taxis

the wind outside
blows and blows

taking one satchel
containing underwear
a clean shirt money

and a pistol
he begins to walk

down a dirt road
toward several small
bumps on the horizon

which he correctly
assumes to be

civilization

7. The Age of Progress

speeds down the freeway
making history

evening arrives
but what can he do
with such a thing

nothing exists for him
unless it is advertised

the coyote and quail
did not ask his
permission to live

so he carries a gun
and shoots at close range

he deals in real estate
the mountains fear him more
than they fear an earthquake

they know the deadly god
out of the machine

now troubles the land

DISINTEGRATION

the day after you left
things began to break down
as if they were trying
to tell me something

first the cooler died
without warning
and the dogs accused me
of causing the heat

then it rained
and the roof leaked
so I waded through empty rooms
learning that a mop
speaks only to a bucket
and a bucket speaks to no one

this morning
after the dishwasher drowned
in its own soapy water
all the eggs
fell out of the refrigerator
and lay on the floor
staring up at me
with their broken eyes

now I feel the old
pain in my hip
which has returned and moved in
to take your place

soon the valves of my body
will begin to falter
the intricate webs
of my muscles will unweave
while my teeth slowly loosen
and the lines on my face
go astray

but I would have been
no use without you anyway
what good is one shoe

JOB THE FATHER

I have made my bed in darkness.
—Job 17:13

all his children in the same house
and a great wind comes
out of the wilderness

seven sons three daughters
all his eggs in one basket
and a great wind comes

reading the story I am paper
curling to avoid the flame

and no matter what I ask them
the stars say *yes yes yes*
all over the sky

I have but one son all my children
in one place always

and I am still here Lord
in the desert where even my fear
has grown a little courage of its own

saying *take me Lord*
take only me
and I will forgive you everything

NOVEMBER 1ST

last night
the daughters of ignorance
coupled with the sons of despair
in cars parked by a ruined river
while dreams were finding their way home
in the dark
old dreams
staying on old roads
new dreams falling into ditches

troops were being withdrawn
from one battlefield to another
and the President was about to be reelected
because he kills more than any other
and is the best man for the job
and because he wears a mask
on the back of his head
smiling
and because he lives
where the hair of a telescopic sight
crosses its target

but today is the day of the dead
so this morning
I placed at the feet of unfinished statues
the scars I have salvaged
it's my way of protesting

now I sit in a bar
with the bartender and the cockroaches
pretending I am here on a visit
when I know this is home

like a man with no legs
trying to cross them

99

AT FORTY

I don't remember
where I was going
or how I got here
except for a few moments
in the womb of a train at night

outside the window a moon
and inside a sound
so steady it seemed like silence

it's too late I know
but I keep thinking it will
get earlier I will start
getting younger slowly
and this time doing it backwards
I will do it right

and finally I will
grow smaller and become
a good wise child at last

Check Out Receipt

Allegany College of Maryland - Cumberland
301-784-5269
www.allegany.edu/library/

Wednesday, Oct 23 2013 3:18PM

Item: 30597002157419
Title: Damaged : a novel
Material: Circulating Book
Due: 11/06/2013

Item: 30597002220548
Title: The coldest winter ever : a novel
Material: Circulating Book
Due: 11/06/2013

Item: 30597002065455
Title: Tar baby
Material: Circulating Book
Due: 11/06/2013

Item: 30597000319706
Title: Selected poems, 1969-1981
Material: Circulating Book
Due: 11/06/2013

Total items: 4

Thank You!

LETTER TO A DEAD FATHER

Five years since you died and I am
better than I was when you were living.
The years have not been wasted.
I have heard the harsh voices
of desert birds who cannot sing.
Sometimes I touched the membrane
between violence and desire
and watched it vibrate.
I learned that a man
who travels in circles
never arrives at exactly the same place.

If you could see me now
side-stepping triumph and disaster,
still waiting for you to say *my son*
my beloved son. If you could only see
me now, you would know I am stronger.

Death was the poorest subterfuge
you ever managed, but it was permanent.
Do you see now that fathers
who cannot love their sons
have sons who cannot love?
It was not your fault
and it was not mine. I needed
your love but I recovered without it.
Now I no longer need anything.

THE PRINCES OF EXILE

stand near the gates of the desert
and watch for travelers who pass by.
When they see a familiar face
they turn aside and remain at a distance.
Instead of the music of home they hear
a foreign wind singing
to trees which bear no leaves.

The Princes of Exile move
through languages and are refracted,
dragging their crippled shadows
beneath an alien sun. They wear
masks of greeting. When they
close their eyes, no one can see them.

The Princes of Exile pray
for sleep and that each day
will be shorter than the last.
They go to bed with the passionate
daughters of strangers and are unsatisfied.
They lie awake trying to name
stars they do not recognize.

When a traveler crosses the border
between foreign countries,
he shifts a burden from one hand
to the other. When he crosses
the border into his own land,
he removes a pebble from his shoe.

The Princes of Sacrifice return
as rain in a drought year.
The Princes of War return
as sores on the faces of politicians.
The Princes of Betrayal return
impaled on the swords of their friends.
But the Princes of Exile never return.

THE STONES

I love to go out on summer nights and watch the stones grow. I think they grow better here in the desert, where it is warm and dry, than almost anywhere. Or perhaps it is only that the young ones are more active here.

Young stones tend to move about more than their elders consider good for them. Most young stones have a secret desire which their parents had before them but have forgotten ages ago. And because this desire involves water, it is never mentioned. The older stones disapprove of water and say, "Water is a gadfly who never stays in one place long enough to learn anything." But the young stones try to work themselves into a position, slowly and without their elders noticing it, in which a sizable stream of water during a summer storm might catch them broadside and unknowing, so to speak, and push them along over a slope or down an arroyo. In spite of the danger this involves, they want to travel and see something of the world and settle in a new place, far from home, where they can raise their own dynasties away from the domination of their parents.

And although family ties are very strong among stones, many have succeeded; and they carry scars to prove to their children that they once went on a journey, helter-skelter and high water, and traveled perhaps fifteen feet, an incredible distance. As they grow older, they cease to brag about such clandestine adventures.

It is true that old stones get to be very conservative. They consider all movement either dangerous or downright sinful. They remain comfortably where they are and often get fat. Fatness, as a matter of fact, is a mark of distinction.

And on summer nights, after the young stones are asleep, the elders turn to a serious and frightening subject—the moon, which is always spoken of in whispers. "See how it glows and whips across the sky, always changing its shape," one says. And another says, "Feel how it pulls at us, urging us to follow." And a third whispers, "It is a stone gone mad."

104

THE GREAT GULF

Between us and you there is a great gulf fixed: so that they which would pass from hence to you cannot; neither can they pass to us, that would come from thence. —*Luke 16:26*

1

At night when each dark shape in the desert
glows in the light of its own penumbra
I take the road by one white hand
and lead it to a deep arroyo, a dry wash
in which the river lives when it is home.
Stones remain where the water dropped them
and beneath them aged scorpions sleep
in small hotels with no view at all.
The sand is cool. I wonder if the river
will be here when I need to drown.

2

We choose from what is available and fall
in love: anchorites with spiders, sailors
with each other; the bleeding foot
returns to embrace the shattered glass;
the overdose goes in search of an addict;
and those who are too much afraid
fall in love with their fear.

3

I was broken by love but I was
so well repaired I can pass for anybody,
standing here where a river used to be.
In one hand my prayers, in the other the answers,
with a great gulf fixed between them.

To get here I dragged my shadow
over sharp stones and felt its cuts
and bruises. But the river was dry.

Oh Jesus Christ
and all my fingers losing their rings!
What will become of me when I offer
my soul to the Devil and he doesn't
want it? What will I do
when there is no one left to betray?

THE MONSTER

I have a singular talent: the ability to make old women cry. Whenever I see one, I say to her, "Something is lost and since it was never here and I have never seen it, I despair of finding it. Please help me! There is no one else for me to turn to."

She begins to search frantically, not knowing for what, and she finds various things. A darning egg, a bus token, a stiffened shoe, a ceramic bird. And she holds these things up to me one by one, saying, "Is this it? Is this?" And each time I shake my head sadly.

Sooner or later she comes upon the one thing she has hidden from herself, the thing she has successfully forgotten. A tiny spoon, a necklace with a broken clasp, a sea shell. And when she finds it, she begins to cry.

SURVIVAL

1

In April summer arrives
facedown. The sun is cruel
but not as cruel as the moon
whose mad face offers comfort.
To be comforted by such a moon
is to walk barefoot through groves
of crippling cholla, scourged
by ocotillo, and crouch all night
in a dry arroyo, howling
like a coyote in search of love.

2

A chaparral hen nests
in the palo verde, alert and still.
Her mate watches from the false
nest they have built to fool
their enemies. Tonight a coyote
is a dark haze five feet
below them. They do not move
or blink their eyes. A rabbit
screams. The glowing shadow
moves past with something dripping
from its mouth. Another shadow stops
to lick the stones, then follows.

3

Three months without rain.
Crazed with thirst, the quail
peck at bits of clear glass
beside the road. Coyotes
and great cats can quench
their thirst with blood, but where
can the deer find water? What
nourishes the lichen on these stones?

Nature at the mercy of nature,
and man without mercy, the nature
of man. I am secondary
among the primary sources, trying
to save myself from love and other
dangers, trying to hold still.

4

Watched closely by the birds,
I gather the things a man needs
to build his strange nest:
stones for a wall, sand
for mortar, the ribs of dead
saguaros for a roof. A dry
country is for those who choose it,
for those who are fragile
and beat down by such gentle rain.

Today a hot wind wrung me dry.
It died at sunset. Now the road
is white as lime and the desert bleaches
under the moon, all bone and shadow,
the floor of a star-filled sea.

Comfort me with anything but the moon:
salt for a cracked lip, an old
shirt which has lost my shape
but remembers my odor. I know
where my edges are, where I cease
and the desert night begins.

I never broke the rules; the rules
broke me. If I wear protective
coloring, the costume of survival,
it is because I was not equipped
with sharp enough teeth. I have
seen the gods and they are ruthless.

COMFORT

do not worry
the snow will melt
the roads will again be passable
these delays are temporary
those who left you will come back

the spilled milk will be replaced
and the doll's missing blue eye
will be sewn on in exactly the right place

the hand of darkness you held all night
which slipped from you at dawn
will come over the horizon
reaching for your hand
and the pain will return

DRY SEASON

1

some years the birds
fly south for the winter
and there isn't any

trees beckon to them
but they fly into the desert
which has had no autumn rain

it is late October in a dry season
the coyotes are warming up
for a night of unearthly music
and the moon hangs
by its horns
above the Santa Ritas

I am trying to say something
about my life
in a dry season
while thirsty birds sleep
with their heads under their wings
and coyotes chant *vanity*
vanity vanity

2

when a man loves the desert
he loves it
as he loves a woman

at first in spite of
her imperfections
and later because of them

3

all day I lifted stones
and fitted them into a wall
carrying each one carefully
walking on my heels
like a woman with child

the wall will stand
perhaps five years
before the stones leave me

when they have made
their journeys down slopes
and into deep arroyos
I will slip out and find them
scarred and chipped
in the moonlight
and bring them home

4

there is a bird
who follows me
curious to know what I am doing
and why should he fear me
when he kills rattlesnakes
and outruns coyotes

there is a spider
who struggles so hard
to escape the embrace
of his huge lovesick mate
that he dies of exhaustion

there is a toad
who digs his way six feet up
toward the desert rain
and when he arrives
bleats like a lamb

5

I have chosen this place
and given it a name
it is called my place

a place without subtlety
where morning light
is unfiltered by leaves and the wind
blows unhampered by leaves

where sunlight hurls itself down
as if each day
would be followed by two nights

sunlight which pierces
the closed eyelid
and impales the eye

and after a day heavy with heat
in which to be empty-handed
is burden enough
the sudden vacuum of dry cold

6

now while the moon pulls darkness
toward a place where somebody
must need it more than I do

114

and new stones
are struggling slowly
to the surface
I wait with the chollas
who stand under the shelter
of their dangerous long blond hair
and watch for rain

7

I who was promised
little by men
have waited for it gone without
in order to have it
and finally it arrives
as a blessing

place I have chosen
where I will not pay tribute
to those from whom
I learned the most

if they want it they must
steal it from me as I
stole their knowledge from them

place I have chosen
where exile is home

thicken my roots and extend them
toward secret compartments
of dark water
which will nurture me
that I might live
a life without explanation
in all the books of men

115

STRANGER

do not be afraid
of the emptiness around you.
If you remain here,
your eyes will grow accustomed
to desert light.

Then you will be able
to distinguish between seasons.
You will begin to see
the citizens of this country
and realize you are not alone.

As each sun rolls over you
on its journey west,
you will grow
quieter with listening
until you can hear the dry
whispers of scorpions,
and the mountains grinding
against one another with desire.

The cloudless sky
will send all shadows
to places of refuge, but you will
live on the head of a pin
where your needs are balanced
and night comes as a knife
so sharp you feel no pain
but there is a new scar
every morning.

If you give the scars a home
and cherish them,
you will become silent
and worthy of exile, and beautiful
beyond all witnessing.

NAVAJO SONG

Where one mountain sits on top of another
we turn the basket upside down
and sing a holy song.

> *We are in great peace.*
> *We are in great peace.*

It is not true
but it will confuse our enemies,
and none can sing the dead back again.

The little bat sits in the last row
with his coat over his head.
Take our pain and put it into the fire.

> *We are in great peace.*
> *We are in great peace.*

When you ask for something
you must give something in return,
but none can sing the dead back again.

LOCAL KNOWLEDGE

For Michael Hogan

on December nights
when the rain we needed months ago
is still far off and the wind
gropes through the desert
in search of any tree to hold it

those who live here all year round
listen to the irresistible
voice of loneliness
and want only to be left alone

local knowledge is to live in a place
and know the place
however barren

some kinds of damage
provide their own defense
and we who stay in the ruins
are secure against enemies and friends

if you should see one of us
in the distance as your caravan passes
and if he is ragged and gesturing
do not be mistaken

he is not gesturing for rescue
he is shouting *go away*

SONORA FOR SALE

this is the land of gods in exile
they are fragile and without pride
they require no worshipers

we come down a white road in the moonlight
dragging our feet like innocents
to find the guilty already arrived
and in possession of everything

we see the stars as they were years ago
but for us it is the future
they warn us too late

we are here we cannot turn back
soon we hold out our hands
full of money
this is the desert
it is all we have left to destroy

WONDERS OF THE WORLD

light is a vehicle for shadows
darkness brings only itself

mountains and continents
rising falling
the earth breathes slowly

the river always moving on
the sea always trying to get out

it is cold and they are naked
but the trees catch snow
in their hands

the rain in all its moods
still anonymous

the star in the apple
the nest in the pomegranate
the maze in the onion

ONE MORE TIME

And he took the blind man by the hand, and led him out of the town; and when he had spit on his eyes, and put his hands upon him, he asked him if he saw ought. And he looked up, and said, I see men as trees, walking. —Mark 8:23–24

with my hat on backwards
to salute the sun
which rises behind me

with my incredible consistencies
a shoebox full of cloves and absences
and an anguished letter from my friend
the misunderstood flute
I am moving on

wearing time thin on my shoulders
a little naked hope and not enough
hair to cover my head

I am moving on
with the dentist's bill in my mouth
my teeth in my pocket
and my ticket
in the coat I left in the closet

with the pain in my hip
like a splintered leg I have walked on
so long I know every tooth
in the bone
with my bottle of whiskey and the pain
like a baby I drug and rock
in its cradle all night
saying for God's sake
go to sleep

with the ghost of the father I loved
who could not love me
now holding my hand

121

and a good woman who was foolish enough
to take me and keep me
not out of charity
but out of her still unsatisfied need
I have survived

I trusted the blind possibilities
and we groped our way
expecting no miracles no
undeserved spittle of Christ

but if it were offered
I would take the journey again
out of darkness through darkness
into darkness
if it were offered
I would take the same journey again

I HAVE NO WINGS

but since I have feet I can walk
since I can walk I will arrive
and when I arrive the place will be there

if there are stairs I will climb
if there is water I will swim
if there are words I will speak

when I am desired I will be chosen
when I am chosen I will take my place
when no one is near me I will be alone

a tired man carries only himself
a frightened man carries himself and his shadow
a vicious man carries the weight
of all he would harm

a loud voice is a stranger in any land
if there is silence let me guard it
a low voice rules its own country
if there is love let me hold it
a small room is enough to contain me
if there is hope let me give it a home

DEAR LIFE

if I use my imagination
I can create a river
where I can fish
swim or drown myself
there are always choices

after I have eaten a bad meal
I do not demand my hunger back
nor do I expect the night
to be less cold
because I lack a coat

pain is a room I measure
each time I am in it
and each time I leave
I forget its dimensions

the wind blows over the desert
telling me nothing
but when I forget the force
to which broken stones complain
I will be lost

when I cannot feel the vine's
need to hold onto something
or when I am happy
only in the presence of others
I will be lost

to the God of Joy
or the God of Sadness
I could tell everything
and each would accept my story
and claim me for his own

but to the God of Remorse
I have nothing to say
and no time to say it

I am holding on for dear life
as my chariot rolls
into the future
faster than I would have thought
possible on its square
wooden wheels

WHATEVER BECAME OF ME

1

because the moon comes
straight up from the mountain
like the hidden possibility of madness
escaped for everyone to see

and the wandering stars
who are said to rule our lives
wander on in darkness

I feel a need to lie down among the stones
and caress any of them
who have survived

2

I always looked for what I wanted
in the wrong places
until the desert
taught me to want what I found

now on summer nights
I sit in the garden
where it is hot and dry
and young stones grow like weeds

when the moon turns
a mad white face upon me
having nothing to offer I hold up
my empty hands
it is so easy to be happy

3

this morning a woodpecker woke me
practicing on his drum
and all afternoon cicadas rang
like the telephones I haven't answered

I am what has become of me
a man who lives in the desert

where coyotes wail more skillfully
than hired mourners
at the funeral of an Eastern king

where every night the stars
whose light I have not earned
and will never deserve
return as if to keep a promise

and even the rain
when it falls is coming home

From

The Bus to Veracruz

1978

Pain

the biggest bore in town
arrives at my party.
as if he were invited

and begins to tell me
the details of what a terrible
time he had getting there

but it was worth it he says
and I know he will be
the last to leave

MEXICO

once each year
after a warm day in April
when darkness comes to the desert
uninvited but planning to spend the night
something hits me like a shovel
and I am stunned into believing
anything is possible

there is no overture to frenzy
I simply look up and see Scorpio
most dangerous of friends
with the last two stars in his tail
blinking like lights at a railroad crossing
while in one claw he holds the top
of a mountain in Mexico

and suddenly I know
everything I need is waiting for me
south of here in another country
and I have been walking through empty
rooms and talking to furniture

then I say to myself
why should I stay home and listen to Bach
such precision could have happened
to anyone to an infinite number
of monkeys with harpsichords

and next morning I start south
with my last chances flapping their wings
while birds of passage stream over me
in the opposite direction

I never find what I am looking for
and each time I return older
with my ugliness intact
but with the knowledge that if it isn't there
in the darkness under Scorpio
it isn't anywhere

MY HANDS ARE MY ENEMIES

they want to caress
every beautiful face and body
we pass on the street

I conquer them I make them reach
for a doorknob pick up a pencil
open a book

but at night
when they take off my shoes
they tell each shoe
to wait for its lover in the dark

I have put my face into my hands
trying to forget it
but they reminded me
it was still the same face

I have picked up my name
like a frightened bird
and held it gently in my hands
begging them to let me keep
this fragile thing
as a pet
but my hands opened
and the bird flew away

I have trusted my scarred hands
but they have not been
faithful to me

and sometimes
when they think I am not looking
one of them takes
the other in its arms
whispering *hold me hold me*
what we wanted was always
beyond our reach
otherwise
we would not have wanted it

LANDSCAPE WITH A WOMAN

when shadows climb
out of the desert
up the sides of mountains
and violent birds pass like projectiles
on their way home for the night
I say I have given you
everything it was all I had

when darkness rises
to the tops of the saguaros
and a river of cool air begins to flow
down the arroyo
I say I have given you
little it was all I had

when the moon
sits on top of the Santa Ritas
then levitates becoming smaller
and more pale as it goes
I say I have given you
nothing it was all I had

but you do not listen you go on
into your losses without birds
without mountains or shadows
or the moon you look into yourself
and say it is not enough
it was never enough

135

GUILT

you led me through cactus
all the way without shoes
leaving a trail wide enough
for anyone to follow
and the dogs with their noses
trained for blood

but if I hadn't known
where you lived
I couldn't have found you
here beyond the words
beyond the confession

guilt
among the strings
of whose harp I have blundered
as the crow flies
as the moon rises
expecting harmony to happen
by accident expecting
tired old men to emerge
from the village and say
we are glad you have come

and finding disgust
the perfect gift
the sweater you made for me
which does not fit but I will
wear it always
to please you

TO MY OTHER SELF

when the warnings
have fallen into the wrong hands
never to be heard of again
and the Church of the Holy
Innocents is empty
we will meet where atheists
come to pray and believers
curse God and die

while the saw moves
and the wood says *thank you*
thank you thank you to its torturer
we will turn upon one another
with our knives dulled
in the service of banality

we will hear a snake gliding
through feathers and see
the hawk circling
with his eye on the sparrow
and we will know for one moment
exactly what is happening
and that it is happening to us

when the screams begin it will be
too late and when they cease
it will be much later
we will lie down together
and I will hold you hold you
in my bloody arms and each of us
will say to the other *I did it for you*
because I love you I did it for you

THE BOOJUM TREE

The dog days of marriage have come
and gone for another year.
What is left of the raddled moon
stays up later than it did
and all its complaints are legitimate.
The prickly pear is shriveled
from lack of water. Its fruit
turns from the color of new blood
to the color of old blood
and drops away.

The worst is over. Through it all
the birds did not sing, but called
to one another: Are you there?
Are you there? And each afternoon
the clouds arrived on schedule,
bringing no rain.

During those days we learned
that the desert is not a metaphor.
I am punished for your sins,
and you are punished for mine.
Now the hideous boojum tree
grows upside down between us,
an insane turnip. We have learned
not to trust one another, never
to trust anyone who is
dying of thirst.

A BIRD IN THE HAND: TWO SOLOS

Wife: there was nothing wrong with our dreams
           they fit us like scales on a fish

           our dreams of patience and goodness
           were not beyond our abilities
           and our dreams of sex were harmless

           there was nothing
           wrong with our dreams except
           they were the wrong dreams for us

           now we see we had little choice
           and once we had chosen each other
           even that was taken away

Husband: when I reached out with my right hand
           and touched you
           I knew everything had been planned
           even what I am saying now
           had been prepared
           for me to say

           and if I had reached out
           with my left hand
           at a different time on a different day
           you would have been there
           and everything would be the same

Wife: coming of age
           I found myself in the desert
           following the wrong leader
           but how could I have abandoned you
           when I knew you would perish without me

139

so I said let it ride
and I rode with it
through a godforsaken land without trees
or flowers or anything beautiful
while the wind played my ribs like a harp

I don't enjoy being laughed at
but I have learned
to practice a certain amount of madness
most difficult of the arts
and the least rewarding

Husband: before we realized what they were
they were over
those days when we lived
in furnished rooms and could laugh
at their ugliness

later
well on our way
and established in our own shambles
drinking good wines and eating good salads
we gave up bread and butter
and those private days those brief
beautiful days

gladly
as if we had a choice

Wife: I keep busy all day
but when the sun goes down
I seem to go with it

140

once I walked out the door and entered night
because it was there
and because it promised everything
but what became of the promises
we didn't live up to

only the young are aware of life
burning at their shoulders
only they know his touch

later it is all speculation
and empty phone booths
waiting for violent acts of love

I keep telling myself I will
feel better tomorrow
but I don't believe it
there is always tomorrow night

Husband: I saw you sleeping
knees bent to the right a little apart
head turned to the left
right arm at your side and left arm
above your head with your hand
caught in the wildness of your hair

until I saw you like that
I never understood why
there were so many paintings of nudes

Wife: we are separate people
each what he fears most each his own
trap his own bait his own victim
I am not responsible for your life
and you are not responsible for mine

141

I wanted to get married
and you thought that meant I loved you

now you are going deaf and I pity you
how hard it must be for a man
who has been blind all these years

Husband: there are others
who had all the advantages I had
and kept them
but deafness grows
on my family tree like a vine
choosing one limb and avoiding another

now that my ears
have started to go blind
I find myself among the chosen
and someday I will hear the true sound
of darkness

I have learned to expose my eyes
to the lips of strangers
and understand what they cannot say

living as I do
with my secrets unheard
and listening always with my eyes
how can I blame you
if you turn your face away

Wife: all afternoon
your shadow your only child
grew taller

now he is leaving and you will be alone
in the darkness that has been
and the darkness that is coming
the same darkness

bright moons in the blood move on
as water moves in the bed of a river
sleeping at night and waking
somewhere else

once I turned quickly and saw you
looking only at me

even if I could explain I wouldn't
even if I could explain to you
I would oh I would

how any love story is a sad story
and we kiss ourselves goodby
each time we kiss each other

Husband: those who have no children
become the children they were
and those who have several children
extend themselves like fingers
stretching into deep grass

but we have only one child
and both of us must crowd into his body
elbowing each other for space

Wife: I remember
when this photograph was taken

143

the aperture opened on my life
as it was as it appeared to be
with the eyes of a deer on the wall
and a tongue which could tell
the truth
but the other was easier

my life created for me
and I like a fool accepted it
with its hand over its mouth
to hide the bleeding

waiting on the steps
of the front porch for years saying
you are young you will find somebody

my life with a life of its own
daring me to leave it
saying I am all I have it isn't enough

Husband: waiting is hardest but we have to wait
for the good things to come to us

I always have this next thing to do
while I am waiting
something important that needs to be done
a dog to be fed a plant to be watered

I had two friends
one is gone the other is dead
now our son is grown up and no longer
needs me and you say I am the cause
of all your unhappiness

these things are true
but there is always this next
thing to do something important
that needs to be done while I am waiting

Wife: ambition
worm in my bowels
the more I starve you the more you grow

others have killed their thousands
but you have killed your tens of thousands

I tell you
the stars can see only into the past
they do not know what I am doing
and do not care and the moon
which knows everything
cares even less

but you answer me with the story
about water always running away from home
and returning purified

Husband: years ago I took this woman
you took this man
and we kept each other
but each of us still wants to be a victim
as if love were an accident
caused by carelessness
and we could hold one another responsible

in order to get what we need from each other
what have we traded except parts of our lives
huge parts of our lives

145

and what have we gained
except huge parts of each other's lives
love always gives
more than we bargain for

Wife: I heard a bird cry a name
and when I looked I found you
in the trap of my hand
crying a name I could not understand
your own or the name of someone you lost
it was never mine

I tried to find someone to love me
before it was too late
but there was no one

Husband: I heard a bird call my name
but when I found the bird
it was you
caught in the trap of my hand
and what I heard was your pain
it has always been

I tried to find a place
where I could not hear that sound
but there was no place

Wife: *I heard a bird cry a name*
Husband: I heard a bird call my name
         and when I looked
                it was you
         in the trap of my hand
                what I heard was your pain
         crying a name I could not understand
                it has always been
         your own or the name of someone you lost
                it was never mine
         I tried to find
                a place
         someone to love me
                but there is no other place
         there is no other one

147

THE PROPHET

recognized by the others
because his dog did not bark
identified and branded
citizen of neither country
he was banished and left behind
to guard the passes

where flowers dry
from natural causes and hang on
to be tormented by the wind
which goes by with some
destination in mind
but unsure of the right direction

and each morning
while stars flee for their lives
he remains and looks toward the east
knowing the sun would rise there
if it could

THE ANGEL AND THE ANCHORITE

For an angel went down at a certain season into the pool, and troubled the water: whosoever then first after the troubling of the water stepped in was made whole of whatsoever disease he had. —John 5:4

1

when the road forked
he took the middle way
and disappeared into the desert
but the pattern of the life he avoided
emerged as a birthmark on his hand

late one night he cut off the hand
carried it into a village
and left it
on the doorstep of the only house
with a light still burning

the note said *take care of my child*
it is an ugly thing
but I cannot bear to kill it

he hid at the edge of the road
and watched her open the door
he could not see her face
but in the light from the doorway
she seemed to be wearing a halo
as she knelt down quickly
taking his hand unwashed and bloody
into her slender arms

2

on the evening of the third day
when no miracle happened
he knew he would die soon

the road rose before him like a ladder
and he began to climb toward her
gripping each rung
with the only hand he had left

she found him outside her door
she touched his wound and said
this is where I was taken from
she put on his makeshift solitudes
and wore them like widow's weeds
she became the angel
who troubled his waters

3

each morning he rolls over
rising to the surface facedown
and she tries with all her strength
to revive him but he is lost
still wandering through the desert
hearing the stones' dry whispers

she watches him drift in his sleep
into another life
she cannot wake him
and she fears there will not be
enough of him left to love

when a white moon rises
with one edge frayed to nothing
an apparition for the dogs to bark at
darkness calls him
like a prayer he can hear
but cannot answer

he feels the wind
blowing through that part of him
which is missing
he hears a lost child
crying for him and he calls out
here here I am but it passes him
stumbling on through the desert

he knows he must meet himself someday
under the only tree on the horizon
and he fears that meeting
more than he fears
thirst or the scorpion

4

the stars point in all directions
and say *go quickly* but she circles
with one wing pinned to him

she no longer believes what he says
his lips are a perfect pair of liars
each verifying the other's
false story
but his hand is honest and has no ally

he says *do not love me*
I cannot carry your pain forever
he says *all we need to survive is patience*
and later we will need nothing

he sees the bridges
washed out between them and everywhere
but tomorrow arrives as if by water

5

they have lived together for twenty years
and they stand beside each other
almost transparent with suffering
they have become the color
of certain feathers
the color of one another

sometimes at night when the moon
rises full of hope and false information
and the acacia is juggling
thousands of tiny golden balls
they walk into the desert
knowing they will not go far
but they will go all the way together

at those times her eyes are luminous
with the fear of darkness
and of this desert place
which has never been her home

he takes one of her hands in his
and leads her into the night
he says *go carefully here my darling*
some of the stones are broken
but they are my friends

he will repeat this as long as he lives
and she will not believe him

THE NEGATIVE VIRTUES

loneliness
is a luxury beyond the reach
of those who have no privacy left
and live in the hope
of its constant invasion
but to those
who have always been alone
it is a friend

poverty
gives us a sense of direction
when we don't know which way to go
and when we walk
on the edge of its cliff
we never go mad we can't afford to

fear
like courage and charity
begins at home and expands in circles
rocking all the boats it touches
and bringing in its wake
the last of the negative virtues

maturity
which is not what we wanted
but comes anyway when we realize
that the things we feared
as children
can no longer hurt us
and that we fear them no less

THE HEAVEN OF THE POOR

Blessed are the poor in spirit:
for theirs is the kingdom of heaven.
—*Matthew 5:3*

through the needle's eye
we can see them
clamoring to get in
each offering to give up what he
cherishes most
not knowing he has become
what he cherishes most

we who are here
had nothing to give up
except our vanity and that
was not required
how can a weak man give up
his strength
or an ugly woman her beauty

in the heaven of the poor
the past keeps going away but is
never quite gone
I was young I was
so young I thought I would
get over it
and all I have learned
is that we never get over anything

some of us were born
to look for a child who has no legs
and wants only to dance
and when we find that child
we take it in our arms
like a flame
and dance and dance

among bricklayers and lawyers
and even poets there are
good people
who work alone
at honest and difficult professions
debauched by others

their reward
will be the heaven of the poor

when they see
the wormholes in the statues
and realize there are kings
who need no followers and have none
they will begin to escape
from the world

each of them will come to a river
and how he gets across it
if he gets across it
will be how he learns to swim

when he crawls out
wet and exhausted on this side
he will look back and see
the bridges he did not know he had
burning burning

---

there are no cities
in the heaven of the poor
no families no friends

we do not pray for what we want
nor do we pray for salvation
we have already
been saved and each night
our dreams show us what we wanted
and could never become

some of us walk on an empty beach
leaving no footprints
and others live
alone in the desert
accepting the rain as love

we do not call it happiness
exactly but we have the moon
to talk to and it always
answers us

do you believe me about the moon
do you think I care
whether or not you do

THE KINGDOM OF THE MOON

in the desert
it is not the sun
we get to know best
but the moon

we learn about it
when we are very young
and not a moment too soon

———◆•••◆———

if you come here to stay
do not worry about
what will happen to you

the moon will take care of you
you will obey it
and the worst will happen

———◆•••◆———

it is no use
asking the moon
philosophical questions

when it tells us anything
it tells us everything
always more
than we wanted to know

———◆•••◆———

the moon commands the desert cold
a word so harsh
it splits the tongue
of the true aloe

the moon pulls stones
to the surface
and directs the ghosts
of dry rivers in their paths
toward the sea

the moon rules the wind
which will fall in love
with anyone
and run away but the moon
brings it back each time
without recriminations

————◄•••►————

at night my shadow
follows me through the desert
like a faithful snake

but it is not faithful to me
it is faithful to the moon

————◄•••►————

other moons can be seen in other places
but the desert moon lives here
and it lives alone

its own friend its own company
its own comfort in the dark

THE VOICE OF THE MOON

When I wake in the night
troubled and thinking
I heard the cry of a bird,
I go to the window
and look out.

Then I realize
it was the cry of the moon.

————◆•••◆————

Years ago I thought
I heard the voice of mountains
which spoke only at night.

Since then I have listened
many times, and I was mistaken.
It was the echo
of the voice of the moon.

————◆•••◆————

When I am unhappy
the moon reminds me
that all things change.

When I am happy
it does the same thing.

————◆•••◆————

I can believe that men
have walked on the moon.
Men would do a thing like that.
But when I am told the moon
is a huge round stone
which does not change its shape
and has no light of its own,
I cannot believe it.

I have heard the voice of the moon.

—◆••◆►—

When I become confused
and do not know who I am,
I listen to the voice of the moon.

The moon knows who everyone is
and forgives all of us.

—◆••◆►—

When the moon is new
it begins at the beginning
and tells the same story
straight through to the end.

It is a long story
but we listen and believe.
Who can doubt
the voice of the moon.

—◆••◆►—

It is important
to learn the habits of the moon.

Otherwise, one might wait
all night and it would not appear.
And when the sun rose triumphant,
one might despair,
believing the moon had been
destroyed and would never return.

———◆◆◆◆▶———

The sun is like fire.
It takes what it wants
and pays no attention to anyone.

But the moon knows each of us.
It looks into our eyes
and remembers all our names.

———◆◆◆◆▶———

When we watch the sun go down
we are impressed with its glory.

When we watch the moon go down
we want to go with it.

———◆◆◆◆▶———

The sea, the wind, and the owl
try to imitate
the voice of the moon,
but none succeed.

Beethoven and Debussy tried
to write its song but compared
with the voice of the moon
one of them created the sound
of screen doors slamming,
and the other, the sound
of a pork chop being fried.

———◆◆◆◆▶———

When the moon rises
in the afternoon and sets
too early to be of any use,
I remember how old I am
and that I no longer
have the option of dying young.

When I sleep and moonlight
comes through the window
and touches me,
I become a dream.

———◆•••◆———

No man turns into a wolf
when the moon is full.

But wolves howl
when the moon is full
because they hear its voice.

———◆•••◆———

Some think the moon is silent.

They are blind.

FIVE LIES ABOUT THE MOON

1. The Full Daytime Moon

She is a bald-headed woman. When someone
shouts "Fire!" she rushes from the building
without her wig. She becomes confused
in the crowd and turns down the wrong street.
We try not to look at her, pale and fragile
as a lost button in search of a shirt.

2. The Waning Crescent Moon

She is young and elegantly thin. She goes
to many parties but does not dance,
preferring to drape herself across a couch
where she is always surrounded by men.
Any of them would gladly place his neck
beneath her delicate foot. She is in love,
nobody knows with whom, and it is hopeless.
When she smiles sadly, they are overcome.
She goes home early and alone.

3. The Half-Moon

She loved her husband. The day he left her
for another woman, one side of her face
became paralyzed. Now she turns that side
away and faces the world bravely in profile.
It is unfair that she, of all women,
should have a Roman nose and a weak chin.

4. The Gibbous Moon

She has lost both her money and her figure
and is defenseless, wearing secondhand light.
Still, she does the best she can to keep up
appearances, and goes from place to place
as she did in the past. Often when she
arrives at the proper address,
perspiring and late, nobody is home.

5. The Full Harvest Moon

She wears gold carelessly, because it is
expected, but she glows from within. Although
she has pressing duties to perform, she moves
through the crowd in the palace hall as if
there were no hurry. The men gasp at her beauty
and the women turn pale with chagrin. Without
slowing her progress toward the door, she offers
a sincere word and a special look to each of them.

DESERT

Sometimes the sun is still trying
to get to the horizon
when a daylight moon comes up,
fragile and almost transparent,
the ghost of a white bird
with damaged wings,
blown from its course and lost
in the huge desert sky.
It is the least protected
of all unprotected things.

A little wind goes by
through the greasewood
heading home to its nest
among blue-veined stones
where it will circle three times
and curl up to sleep
before darkness falls
straight down
like a tile from the roof
of a tall building.

There are families of stones
under the ground.
As the young stones grow
they rise slowly like moons.
When they reach the surface
they are old and holy
and when they break open
they give off a rich odor,
each blooming once in the light
after centuries of waiting.

Those who have lived here longest
and know best
are least conspicuous.
The oldest mountains are lowest
and the scorpion sleeps all day
beneath a broken stone.

If I stay here long enough
I will learn the art of silence.
When I have given up words
I will become what I have to say.

THE NEW ROAD

Tonight at the end of a long
scar in the desert a bulldozer
sleeps with its mouth open
like a great yellow beast.

A coyote sits down to watch it
from a safe distance. An owl
questions again and again.
No answer. Someone is building

a new road, a fine road, wide
and smooth. The huge saguaros
in its path have stood here
two hundred years looking up

at the sky. This will be their
last chance to see the moon.
In the morning the yellow beast
will wake up and move toward them.

We believe in movement. We live
in the sanctity of mobile homes.
We are children of those
who created the portable Indian

and moved him from place to place.
Ours is a republic of cylinders
and pistons, a republic of wheels.
Progress moves before us over

the hill and we pursue it as fast
as we can. With our horses
in trailers, our politicians
in limousines, and all our angels

167

on motorcycles, we pursue it.
The world rolls on and these gods
of the desert cannot get out
of its way. They are no use to us.

———————◄•••►———————

I have stroked them until my hands
are bloody, but what comfort
can I offer? They are doomed
and I am tired of being human,

tired of being mad in a mad world.
Now I lay me down in the new road
but to whom can I pray? The owl
has stopped calling. The coyote

gets up and fades away. I will
look at the moon as long as I can.
Then I will sleep in the desert,
helpless in the path of progress,
waiting for the sound of wheels.

REACHING FOR THE GUN

superficial among the superficial
I have come home
it's a crowded neighborhood
and I go over the long list
of things I don't believe in
as if it mattered on this street
what I do or do not believe

the drunks next door
are beating their child again
taking turns at it
I hear screams
and a thud as the child's knees
hit the floor did that hurt
did that does anything

turning away so I cannot
see through the window
I tell myself I don't
believe in people
but I know I believe in pain

the ultimate goodness
the only goodness which lasts
is the ability to forgive
and I don't have it

I don't believe in murder I say
reaching for the gun and wondering
if Hell is where we wake up dead
and realize how much life
we had left that we didn't use

CERTAIN CHOICES

My friend, who was a heroin addict,
is dead and buried beneath trash
and broken bottles in a prison field.

He died, of course, because of the way
he lived. It wasn't a very good way,
but it kept him alive. When it couldn't
keep him alive any longer, it killed him.
Thoroughly and with great suffering.

After he had made certain choices,
there were no others available. That's
the way it is with certain choices,
and we are faced with them so young.

I have few friends, and none of them
are replaceable. That's the way it is
with friends. We make certain choices.

DEATH ROW

have you been to the land of carnivorous birds
where brown leaves hang on all winter
rattling for release and the fences are strands
of blood strung between living scarecrows

a flat land of small farms
where those who cannot afford a river
build their houses beside a dry ditch
and live behind fever's old walls
while the curtains burn at every window
and outside the dogs bark all night

where each tree waits for its rope
while the stars fall away toward morning
and months come out of the future like bullets
striking the last leg of a one-legged
journey the last arm raised
to shield the last pair of eyes

have you been to that land did you
stumble upon it as a tourist how long
did you stay and can you hear them
calling you still can you hear them calling

HARRY ORCHARD

You lived out of town where the land
sloped up to Table Rock. The prison
looked exactly as a prison should,
except for the roses in front: walls
of granite blocks held together
by their own weight and our fear.
We didn't know what went on in there;
we didn't want to know. The river
kept running. Summer brought heat,
winter brought snow. The grounds
outside the prison were always neat
and the roses were magnificent.

Because of you I grew up thinking prisons
were places outside towns where men
who had the knack for it retired
to tend their roses. I was a child
when I first heard your name, and I
thought you had always been an old man
with a cane who came out and knelt down
stiffly, like in church, among the flowers.
And I thought, because you were so good
at growing things, they named an avenue
in our town, *Orchard*, after you.

When you and the state were young
you were convicted of placing a bomb
on the Governor's gate. He came home
and opened it; it was the last gate
he ever opened. There had been a fight
between miners and the owners of the mines.
You were labor. The Governor was on the side
of management. It's strange how times
and governors don't seem to change.

I don't know whether or not you did it;
but I can imagine you hiding among the vines
which covered the wall outside his mansion,
young and terrified, with sticks of dynamite
like a bouquet in your hands. That was
the picture the state's lawyers painted,
but there were questions about who hired you,
questions about two union bosses and a lawyer.
Somebody paid to shut those questions up.

And what did you do? Oh, Harry! Harry!
You know what you did. You got religion
in the county jail, and when they brought
you to the trial, forgave them all: forgave
the union bosses and the owners of the mines,
forgave the State Militia for their guns,
forgave the men who built the bullpen
at Coeur d'Alene, forgave the striking miners
who starved in it, forgave the Governor,
forgave the crooked lawyers, forgave everyone.
You took it on yourself and praised the Lord,
and even Clarence Darrow couldn't help you then.

Harry Orchard, you lived in prison so long
that when they offered you a pardon in old age,
you refused it. By then you couldn't give
that garden up. And I believe what rumor
later said about the prisoners whose bodies
disappeared after they were beat to death
or died from lack of care, how they were buried
by guards after dark in a place no one would
suspect or dare to desecrate. How many
left their cells to feed the flowers?

And I see you still. It is late afternoon.
You are kneeling in a flower bed, a trowel
in your hand, while all your roses flame.

We always build our prisons out of town
so we won't have to look at them. But we
saw yours. Whole families of us drove
out there to see your roses bloom. We also
saw the statue of the Governor, downtown
in front of the State Capitol, its head
and shoulders white with pigeon droppings.
It's still there, on a traffic island.
Only tourists look at it, and never more
than once. At its base some scraggly roses
grow with yellow leaves and hardly any bloom.
Some things even the state can't do.

Harry Orchard, there stands the Governor
with an iron jaw, squat and menacing,
the ugliest thing a schoolboy ever saw.
Somebody blew him up and he went
into the history book we had to read,
but we could never remember his name.
Harry Orchard, we remember yours
because for over fifty years
outside the gates of Hell you grew
the most beautiful roses in all Idaho.
When you died, you went straight into fame.

THE LAST TIME

Schmid, 32, died Sunday in a Phoenix hospital from wounds suffered in an attack in a trusty dormitory at the prison March 20. Dr. Heinz Karnitzchnig, Maricopa County medical examiner, said his autopsy found 47 stab wounds in Schmid's body. He said the most destructive wounds were in a lung and a kidney.
—*Tucson Daily Citizen, April 5, 1975*

I should never have listened. I should
have left you alone in that place.
Dark as it was, it was not as dark
as the place you are now. I wanted
you to be good, but I did not tell you
the good are vulnerable, that no slate
is ever wiped completely clean.

I wanted you to be able to love,
to be able to trust. It took years,
but you learned so well you could trust
anybody. Even me with my platitudes.
Even them with their can openers.

They must have wanted you to die slowly;
they stabbed you so many times and never
touched your heart. We who care most,
who are most ruthless, go for the heart.

When you thanked me for letting you
into my world, I should have known
you could not survive in that world
without your cunning, without your fear.
And when you said I had made you feel
almost beautiful, I should have foreseen
blood on the floor, blood on the ceiling.

175

You were not beautiful when I saw you
the last time, blind and butchered,
trapped in a web of tubes and machines,
unable to speak, unable to do anything
but listen to my words, my lies, my evasions
which dripped into you as if through tubes.
You were my perfect captive audience,
and whose world were you fighting for then?

Oh Paul, when you come back,
as I know you will, with the white rose
of the grave on your shoulder, do not
come to me, please do not come to me.
I have no more help to give, no further
instructions. I am guilty. And I
could not bear to see you that way again.

SOFTLY SOFTLY

For Paul David Ashley

one day in April
when the palo verdes
have become golden beehives
and the acacia is showing
some promise of green
summer arrives in Sonora
full-grown
without remorse
without consulting anybody

on that day
the arms of the ocotillo
bend toward the earth
and at the end of each arm
is a hand filled with blood

every year in the desert
spring dies suddenly
while it is still young
and foolish and beautiful
and I survive

death is a poor child
without a mother or father
how could I turn him away

and once I have taken him
into my arms
and cared for him
I will not be afraid of him
when he returns as a man
still needing me
and calling my name

where the sky is king
no tree grows very tall
and flowers
the colors of dawn and sunset
bloom and fade quickly

when there are no second chances
there is no regret
only sadness
which surrounds us
and carpets our steps
like luxury

those of us who know
we will never come back
from wherever we are going
see the beauty
of the landscape
through which we pass

and when it is too late
life begins again
softly my friend
softly

THE POET AS EQUESTRIAN

For James Wright

with the pale horse
under your right foot
the dark horse under your left
keeping your balance astride
two beautiful animals
between which is death
horseman ride on
past all the places you have ever been

past your childhood's house
with nobody home
where the furniture settled for good
the plumbing died the roof fell in
and the walls and ghosts
hold one another in the rain
horseman ride on
like a leaf from the calendar
torn off by the wind

past your friends
the con men who call you brother
and tell you the secret of the world
a different secret each time
but will desert you
far from the promised land
when you have nothing to carry with you
and nothing to leave behind
still believing them
horseman ride on
where you go you will go alone

179

chosen to survive when you were young
you traded the cow for a sack of beans
and learned to climb
you found the golden harp
that sang the music in your head
you listened to the stones and understood
their darkness and stayed awake
all night waiting
for the resurrection of the light

you will outlive your gifts
and even then horseman ride on
the good do not live forever
and the bad live only a little longer
horseman be stronger and when the crowd
wants entertainment
entertain
take down the harp
from where it hangs and make
its tinny strings the victims
of your ruined hands

for you it will be the long way home
you will never find your way now
to the heaven of the brilliant
lucky poets who die young
and when those who praised you
turn away one by one
ride on ride on
with nothing in your eyes but sadness
and the sun

180

ENCOUNTER

In some small flatland town
a stranger waits for me to arrive by train
and when I step down not knowing
where I am or why I have come
I will recognize him and give him my hand
He will fold my pain like a newspaper
and tuck it under his arm
He will take charge of everything

He will open a car door
I will get in and he will drive
expertly down Main Street out of town
toward open country where the sky
is half the world

As night comes on
we will hear grass beside the road
whispering of its native land
and when the stars bear down like music
I will begin to understand how things
that have never happened before
can happen again

THE BUS TO VERACRUZ

The mail is slow here. If I died, I wouldn't find out about it for a long time. Perhaps I am dead already. At any rate, I am living in the wrong tense of a foreign language and have almost no verbs and only a few nouns to prove I exist. When I need a word, I fumble among the nouns and find one, but so many are similar in size and color. I am apt to come up with *caballo* instead of *caballero*, or *carne* instead of *casa*. When that happens, I become confused and drop the words. They roll across the tile floor in all directions. Then I get down on my hands and knees and crawl through a forest of legs, reaching under tables and chairs to retrieve them. But I am no longer embarrassed about crawling around on the floor in public places. I have come to realize that I am invisible most of the time and have been since I crossed the border.

All the floors are tile. All the tiles are mottled with the same disquieting pattern in one of three muddy colors—shades of yellow, purple, or green. They make me think of dried vomit, desiccated liver, and scum on a pond. The floor of my room is dried vomit with a border of scum on a pond, and like most of the floors it has several tiles missing, which is a great blessing to me. These lacunae are oases in the desert where I can rest my eyes. The nausea from which I suffer so much of the time is not caused by the food or water, but by the floors. I know this because when I sit in the town square, which is covered with concrete of no particular color, the nausea subsides.

The town is small, although larger than it would seem to a visitor—if there were any visitors—and remote. It has no landing field for even small planes, and the nearest railroad is almost one hundred kilometers to the east. The only bus goes to Veracruz. Often I stop at the bus terminal to ask about the bus to Veracruz. The floor of the bus terminal is scum on a pond with a border of desiccated liver, but there are many tiles missing. The terminal is always deserted except for Rafael and Esteban, sometimes sitting

182

on the bench inside, sometimes lounging just outside the door. They are young, barefoot, and incredibly handsome. I buy them *Cocas* from the machine, and we have learned to communicate in our fashion. When I am with them, I am glad to be invisible, glad that they never look directly at me. I could not bear the soft velvet and vulnerability of those magnificent eyes.

"When does the bus leave for Veracruz?" I ask them. I have practiced this many times and am sure I have the right tense. But the words rise to the ceiling, burst, and fall as confetti around us. A few pieces catch in their dark hair and reflect the light like jewels. Rafael rubs his foot on the floor. Esteban stares out the filthy window. Are they sad, I wonder, because they believe there is no bus to Veracruz or because they don't know when it leaves?

"Is there a bus to Veracruz?" Suddenly they are happy again. Their hands fly like vivacious birds. *"¡Si, hay! ¡Por supuesto, Señor! ¡Es verdad!"* They believe, truly, in the bus to Veracruz. Again I ask them when it leaves. Silence and sadness. Rafael studies one of the tiles on the floor as if it contains the answer. Esteban turns back to the window. I buy them *Cocas* from the machine and go away.

Once a week I stop at the post office to get my mail from the ancient woman in the metal cage, and each week I receive one letter. Actually, the letters are not mine, and the ancient woman has probably known this for a long time, but we never speak of it and she continues to hand me the letters, smiling and nodding in her coquettish way, eager to please me. Her hair is braided with colored ribbons, and her large silver earrings jingle when she bobs her head, which she does with great enthusiasm when I appear. I could not estimate how old she is. Perhaps even she has forgotten. But she must have been a great beauty at one time. Now she sits all day in the metal cage in the post office, a friendly apparition whose bright red lipstick is all the more startling because she has no teeth.

183

The first time I entered the post office, it was merely on an impulse to please her. I was expecting no mail, since no one knew where I was. But each time I passed, I had seen her through the window, seated in her metal cage with no customers to break the monotony. She always smiled and nodded at me through the window, eager for any diversion. Finally one day I went in on the pretext of calling for my mail, although I knew there would be none. To avoid the confusion which my accent always causes, I wrote my name on a slip of paper and presented it to her. Her tiny hands darted among the pigeonholes, and to my astonishment she presented me with a letter which was addressed to me in care of general delivery. She was so delighted with her success that I simply took the letter and went away, unwilling to disillusion her.

As soon as I opened the letter, the mystery was solved. My name is fairly common. The letter was intended for someone else with the same name. It was written on blue paper, in flawless Palmer Method script, and signed by a woman. It was undated and there was no return address. But it was in English, and I read it shamelessly, savoring each phrase. I rationalized by convincing myself that the mail was so slow the man to whom the letter had been written was probably already dead and could not object to my reading his mail. But I knew before I finished the letter that I would return to the post office later on the chance there might be others. She loved him. She thought he was still alive.

Since then I have received one letter each week, to the enormous delight of my ancient friend in the post office. I take the letters home and steam them open, careful to leave no marks on the delicate paper. They are always from the same woman, and I feel by now that I know her. Sometimes I dream about her, as if she were someone I knew in the past. She is blond and slender, no longer young but far from old. I can see her long, graceful fingers holding the pen as she writes, and sometimes she reaches up to brush a strand of hair away from her face. Even that slight gesture has the eloquence of a blessing.

When I have read each letter until I can remember it word for word, I reseal it. Then, after dark, I take it back to the post office by a circuitous route, avoiding anyone who might be on the street at that hour. The post office is always open, but the metal cage is closed and the ancient one is gone for the night. I drop the letter into the dead letter box and hurry away.

At first I had no curiosity about what happened to the letters after they left my hands. Then I began to wonder if they were destroyed or sent to some central office where, in an attempt to locate the sender and return them, someone might discover that they had been opened. Still later, the idea that some nameless official in a distant city might be reading them became almost unbearable to me. It was more and more difficult to remember that they were not my letters. I could not bear to think of anyone else reading her words, sensing her hesitations and tenderness. At last I decided to find out.

It took months of work, but with practice I became clever at concealing myself in shadowy doorways and watching. I have learned that once each week a nondescript man carrying a canvas bag enters the post office through the back door, just as the ancient woman is closing her metal cage for the night. She empties the contents of the dead letter box into his canvas bag, and he leaves by the door he came in. The man then begins a devious journey which continues long into the night. Many nights I have lost him and have had to begin again the following week. He doubles back through alleys and down obscure streets. Several times he enters deserted buildings by one door and emerges from another. He crosses the cemetery and goes through the Cathedral.

But finally he arrives at his destination—the bus terminal. And there, concealed behind huge doors which can be raised to the ceiling, is the bus to Veracruz. The man places his canvas bag in the luggage compartment, slams the metal cover with a great echoing clang, and goes away.

185

And later, at some unspecified hour, the bus to Veracruz rolls silently out of the terminal, a luxury liner leaving port with all its windows blazing. It has three yellow lights above the windshield and three gold stars along each side. The seats are red velvet and there are gold tassels between the windows. The dashboard is draped with brocade of the richest shades of yellow, purple, and green; and on this altar is a statue of the Virgin, blond and shimmering. Her slender fingers are extended to bless all those who ride the bus to Veracruz, but the only passenger is an ancient woman with silver earrings who sits by the window, nodding and smiling to the empty seats around her. There are two drivers who take turns during the long journey. They are young and incredibly handsome, with eyes as soft as the wings of certain luminous brown moths.

The bus moves through sleeping streets without making a sound. When it gets to the highway, it turns toward Veracruz and gathers speed. Then nothing can stop it: not the rain, nor the washed-out bridges, nor the sharp mountain curves, nor the people who stand by the road to flag it down.

I believe in the bus to Veracruz. And someday, when I am too tired to struggle any longer with the verbs and nouns, when the ugliness and tedium of this place overcome me, I will be on it. I will board the bus with my ticket in my hand. The doors of the terminal will rise to the ceiling, and we will move out through the darkness, gathering speed, like a great island of light.

Uncollected Poems

Courage

is not based upon ability.
It is extra.

Knowing that somebody
always gets hurt, it gambles
every cent it has
and all it can borrow from friends.

And when it wins,
it gives back everything.
And even when it loses, it wins.

HOW TO AMUSE A STONE

command the stones in a loud voice
or speak to them
just to the left of silence
or sing them a love song in Spanish
they will not respond

write a letter
in it confess all your sins
place it under a stone
leave it there for months
and when you return you will find
your letter unopened and unread

stones have a sense of dignity
greater than that of kings
a sense of honor
stronger than that of friends

stones are fulfilled like prophecy
tendentious as rain
and have a sense of humor
more subtle than we can comprehend

it takes a long time to amuse a stone
first you must capture one
carry it away
imprison it with mortar in a wall
the stone will not complain

then you must wait
and years after you are gone
under another stone on which
some stranger carved your name
the mortar in your wall will crumble
and the stone you captured
will fall to the ground
amused and free and going home

TERRITORIAL RIGHTS

The Gambel quail looks like a medieval knight
in a plumed russet helmet with lowered visor
outlined in white. Every morning in early spring
he flies to the top of a cholla, where he can see
his mate and the boundaries of his territory.
They are monogamous, but at dawn he crows
as proud as any barnyard rooster with a harem.
And she is a lovely thing, plump and demure
in gray and a smooth brown cloche with a plume
which bobs above her head as she gathers her chicks,
nodding to each in turn, always counting them.

Once I saw a pair of Gambels attack
a roadrunner who was threatening their chicks.
Quail seldom fly, but these came in like two
jet planes, low and fast and side by side.
The roadrunner was three times their size. They struck
at exactly the same moment, a maneuver requiring
absolute precision. The stunned roadrunner
fell down. They landed quickly and ushered the chicks
away, calling *hurry now, hurry now.* Tiny shadows
ran after them. By the time the carnivorous
giant had regained his breath, his feet,
and his dignity, the quail were gone.

The pair I know best live in the acacia thicket
at the bottom of the arroyo. They have a nest
on the ground, hidden by cactus and rabbit brush.
If I come too near, he sounds the alarm and they
take cover. If I stay, he comes out to harangue me
and do battle. He threatens me with death or, at best,
banishment from his territory. I hold my ground.

It's my land and my arroyo, I shout at him.
I will not abandon it to a crazy quail.
He tries to lead me away from the nest. I know
he will sacrifice himself if he must. This is
the desert. It has always been his home.
I give up and return to the house where I belong,
learning from my neighbors in the arroyo to claim
no more territory than I am willing to defend.

THREE POEMS
FOR A TWENTY-FIFTH ANNIVERSARY

1. Housecleaning

after returning
all the tools I borrowed
from neighbors and friends
and the books to the library

I am amazed to find
so many things around the house
like you
that really belong here

I had thought
you were on loan and overdue
the fines were mounting into millions
I could never pay them

so for twenty-five years
I looked everyone straight in the eyes
pretending you were mine
and I kept you

2. Building

you built your house
on my wavering sands

I built my house on yours
and we abide

you are afraid of water
I am afraid of winds

you hold me during hurricanes
I keep you from the tide

3. Grandfathering

it is time for grandfathering
and I don't know how
leave me alone I have served my turn
I will run away

then I see your hand
after so many years still pale
and slender as a wand
reach out to touch a child

and I hear you say
when it was time for fathering
you found the way
as you will now

AS I GROW OLDER

I will become smaller
and be able to pass
under the arm of my tall son
who will look down on me

my voice will be thinner
will come from a distant place
deeper inside me

I will grow more subtle
and secretive
quieter each year
tired of bending over the page
down which I run my finger
more and more slowly
in search of the name
and number of the infinite
until in the gray evening light
I will be the evening light

then I can walk out into darkness
becoming the darkness
while the moon
so dead so well preserved
rises through me each night
on its own perfected schedule

LETTING GO

For Brad

you walk down the road
my young and only son
as if everything
were there for your pleasure
and you are right

you pause to touch a tree
and say *alligator juniper*
and again you are right

why should I be surprised
that you have learned
what I have forgotten
and more than I ever knew

my tall bright son
nothing I can do now
will alter the length
of your shadow
as you leave the desert
which has been your home

when you look back
the moon will set
over your shoulder
and the sun will rise
each morning to meet you

turn then
turn away and walk on

nothing I can give you
will forestall
the moment of your death
nor determine how long
how much you will suffer
between this point of light
and that point of light

you have learned
to accept your life
as if it were music
played with great skill
and would last forever
and you are right again
my son my only son
it will last long enough

FACE

you are the mask I was given
and I am what you were given to mask
both of us could have done better
but we had no choice

sometimes late at night
I meet you by accident in the mirror
and you break the silence like a violin
played by a chimpanzee

nothing on your left side
matches anything on your right side
and even if it did you would be
but slightly improved

you go before me
announcing my presence
like a bad omen a harbinger of doom
I keep telling everybody I am
not unhappy it is only my face

and you tell them I am lying
you tell them I am
full of pain and vanity
I am proud and contemptuous
your lips form into a hard line
and you tell them I am growing old
in debauchery

but it is not true
ugly face it is not true

inside me I am
what you could never be
clean featured the eyes are deep-set
and clear the jaw is strong
there is a cleft in the chin
teeth are straight and without gaps

inside me I believe
I have always believed
in a world without freckles
where hair remains faithful to its head
and ears come in matching pairs

POINT OF VIEW

see with the eyes of a horse
whose irises are rows of blue flowers
the world is green and edible

see with the small eyes of a pig
the world is dim and narrow
people are tall and hungry

see with the isinglass eye of an old stove
while the fire in its belly
looks out at a combustible world

see with the eye of a window facing east
light and darkness rising
never coming down again

see with the eyes of a believer
who does not believe what he sees
but sees what he believes

see with the eyes of a painter
who paints what he cannot see
until he has painted it

see with the practical eye of a woman's sex
the world is hard but not durable
fails when most needed

see with the curious eye of a man's sex
many worlds full of mystery
the same secret hidden in each

see with the eyes of a lover
who sees his reflection in a thumbnail
and falls in love

see with the eyes of a prophet
who sees a hammer approaching a thumbnail
and a new nail growing beneath it

see with the bright eye of a lake
the sky and reflect it
the mountains and reflect them

see with the dark eye of a lake
great depths where fish undulate
let that eye go to sleep at night

while the other eye stays open
a trap for the moon

THE MACHINES

how far we had to go
to prove we were capable
circling the machines at first
as though we knew what they were
and could operate them
without practice

and just when we had learned
not well but a little
at least enough to get by
the gods phased out that model
and gave us a new manual

the gods did not laugh at us
they were serious
kindly even paternal
and we were older but still trying
to learn how to work the machines

which became more complex
as they were simplified
more delicate
as they were more efficient
until they ran on their own power
without wheels or gears
and could go on
forever

they directed our hands
with gentle
irresistible pressure
to the correct knobs and buttons
and we were elated
realizing we had learned
to master them at last

201

RESERVATIONS

these bald mountains
have no trees never had any
never knew they were supposed to

such a disappointment
the tourists say *and we came*
all the way from Illinois

the tired tourists are driving
through the reservation
in search of Indians

but the Indians are not reserved
they have painted blue graffiti
on all the water towers

such vulgarity the tourists say
and tell their children
to look the other way

but the sunburned children
grow petulant and noisy
where are the Fuc-ky-ou Indians
the children shout

and keep shouting it
all the way back to Illinois

SONG OF THE HOGAN

In the darkness of the first world
beneath this world
the gray legs of a crow
walk around in search of a body,
saying: At the time when things began
          we knew all about it.
          We knew about the mountain spirit,
          the black sky, the shining stone.
          We knew all about it.

In the silence of the second world
beneath this world
yellow coyotes run in circles
in search of their voices, wanting
to say: At the time when things began
          we knew all about it.
          We knew about the water spirit,
          the corn pollen, the talking god.
          We knew all about it.

In the smoke of the third world
beneath this world
the souls of dead men
carry offerings in search of fire,
saying: At the time when things began
          we knew all about it.
          We knew about all the soft goods,
          the hard goods, the sacred words.
          We knew all about it.

There is no fourth world
beneath this world,
only the fire
          who knows nothing,
          needs nothing, wants nothing
          and is content.

203

A KIND OF GLORY

years after the neighbors
started using machines
Grandpa still did the milking
with his small-boned
delicate hands
but his cows gave better milk
than any herd in the valley

at night he danced the schottische
with Grandma and always
put his little foot right there
more gracefully than she could manage

he smelled of cow manure
and Prince Albert pipe tobacco
women found him irresistible

we knew we would never be famous
or anything out of the ordinary
but for awhile after Grandpa
dropped his flashlight
into the outhouse hole we had
a kind of glory

it continued to shine
straight up from down there
and our most private moments
were illuminated

THE FARMER'S TESTIMONY

The year it didn't rain we waited,
tried the usual things: prayers
and promises, lightning rods, small
planes seeding clouds. The expense
was hideous. Then we tried
the dances. My wife and I danced
all day and night until our feet bled,
our heads buzzed like dying flies
and we fell down in the field
and slept through another dry dawn.

Then the sacrifices began. I don't
rightly know who started them.
We gave the furniture to huge
bonfires and held back only one bed,
the television and the kitchen table.
She cried when I put her mother's
rocker on the fire, but when she saw
our chickens flopping in the place
of sacrifice, the cows going there
one by one, she was quiet and afraid.

Judge me now, my neighbors, as I know
you must. You look at me sideways
and whisper a word. But remember
when it came down to the end and we
stood together in a bloody field, you
gave what was most damaged and least
loved: your senile grandfathers,
your cross-eyed daughters, your half-wit
sons. And all to no avail. I gave
what I prized most, and when I was done
the rains came. She was a good wife.

PROMISES

When America closes for the night
and the last ferryboat leaves Port Townsend,
those of us left behind
cannot remember where it is going.

Low tide hesitates, gathers its strength
and begins to return, bringing driftwood,
seaweed torn up by the roots
and a little light to help us
find our way home. If we were drunker
or younger, we think we might sprawl here
on the beach all night, listening
to the sea's absolute authority
and to foghorns calling each other
like lost and lovesick whales.

But we are no longer boys
who can sleep where we fall and wake
to begin a new journey. We have made
many promises and kept some.
We have wives who are not waiting up
for us but whose eyes will open
no matter how quietly we open the door,
and close again when we close it,
having seen in that moment everything,
understood everything, and forgiven nothing.

AND THE GREATEST OF THESE

All summer while dry winds
ground the grass to chaff
I waited for the sound of water
but when the rains came they were
violent. Now the worst
of the heat is over. At sundown
the earth cools a little.
Mountains to the east turn
expensive and funereal, then darken
like the huge stone ribs of unfinished
cathedrals in Mexico, abandoned
to weather since the Revolution.

As the light dims it seems
that nothing which goes away
will ever return. How far the world
flows out into itself, yet all the pain
I need is here at hand.

Now in the middle of this middle
age, and paying for the gifts
I thought were free, I learn
that what teaches me has taught me
laughter, charity, and pain
of the body: these three
and the greatest of these is pain,
not a question, but the answer
to everything. All other desires
must be forgotten, all other needs
put aside until that lover
has his way with me
and is, for awhile, satisfied.

SONORA WIND

Nobody can stop this dry wind,
this disaster of a wind. Nobody
can heal it, soothe it, send it on.
It remains. Has it nowhere else
to go? Has it been forbidden
to return to where it came from?

It is driving us mad with the sound
of a wound torn open again
and again. It can bend us down
as it bends the greasewood.
It can desiccate our minds.

It screams at us with the voice
of a raging mute who has no words
to tell his pain. When we begin
to scream in return, it rips
the words from our mouths,
replacing them with sand, the taste
of all the evil ever done to us
by those who died before we could
tell them how much we hated them.

THE TEETH OF THESE MOUNTAINS

were worn down
by an ancient inland sea
to whose dry bed we have come
uninvited and unacceptable

the sun which bore down
all day on Sonora is falling
into an ocean far to the west
leaving patches of shadow
trapped in arroyos
and huge wands of color
in the sky

on the east slope
a flash of acacia
greasewood and palo verde
a moment of green light as brief
and precise as a moment of truth

then silence
after the sun's crescendo
cool air after a long fever
the protective walls of darkness
after the phantoms and mirages
of too much light and space

suddenly a cacophony
of coyotes wailing in torment
for the moon to rise
and rescue them from Hell

and a huge tarantula
hauls herself over her threshold
in search of love in search of
a small mate who will not survive
the violence of her embrace

while two young rabbits
huddle under a prickly pear
their eyes opaque with fear
and the great bull snake
having been aloof from the world
for seven days and nights
again feels hunger
and flows out silently
with the perfection of ultimate
grace into his starry kingdom

OUT HERE

when the moon rises
and Sonora is covered
with silence brilliant as snow
I walk into a dream unafraid

down there in the valley
lights go on at night
but out here
the stars are alive and well
and each has a secret name

out here I am alone
but this is my country
well past the halfway point
between the past and future

out here nothing needs me
nothing fails me I lie down
in the bed of an arroyo
look at the stars and forget
first the promises
made to myself kept or broken
then the promises
made to others then my name
place of birth the numbers
and all the rest

when there is nothing left
I remember the precision
of the hummingbird piercing
the dark heart of the hibiscus
and doing no damage

I begin to hear night
breathing through me promising
that death does not last forever
and teaching me
the secret names of the stars

DEATH

has no sense of honor. I challenged him
to battle, win or lose; but when I went
to meet him, he did not appear. Later
I heard his tiny voice whispering in my ear

You carried me to the battlefield
and brought me safely back again.
I have been with you always. I am here.

He followed me like a ghost. I had been told
ghosts could not cross running water, so I went
to the river and swam. When I came out
on the other shore, I saw a dragonfly
above me on the willow branch. Its wings
were fragile and transparent as an angel's.
Again I heard the tiny voice. It said

Thank you for taking me across the water
on your shoulder. Rest on the riverbank.
I will watch over you. Sleep. I will be near.

I slept and dreamed I was the river's
lover; and when I woke, a mist was rising
on the water. The moon came up and everything
was silver. It was more beautiful
than in my dream. I heard the voice again,
this time a murmur, a low wind in the trees.

Someday I will release you from your dreams
of self and pain, and make you part
of all things beautiful. You will be useful
to the earth. Now you call me "Death"
but you will learn my other name
is "Life." We are the same.

TO YOU

Someone is always willing
to deliver the message: the good news,
the bad news, the summons.
He is only a messenger.

He does not leave the battlefield
nor jump from a burning building
to bring you word of those
he left behind. He is not involved.

He picks up the telephone
or rings the doorbell. You have
been elected, failed the test,
there has been an accident.

The message falls
like a brick on your head.
The messenger does not comment.
He is only a messenger.

If the message finds you
on top of the world or buried
in the debris of your failures,
it is all the same to the messenger.

His life is not part of your life.
He is a windmill, taking orders
from the wind. He cannot
control the weather.

His finger on the doorbell
is impersonal. His voice is flat
and even, but you will remember it
the rest of your life. It says:
Anything that can happen
can happen to you.

214

THE LANGUAGE OF POSTCARDS

we are having the wonderful weather
of paradise the last days of a season
which has no beginning nor end
where if I light a cigarette
bougainvillaea will suddenly
flame on every street

shadows of buildings
are fixed in their places
the sky is the famous unfinished
last work of a mad painter
the sea is so calm we forget it
and nobody swims

we are having the wonderful weather
of postcards dead birds fall at our feet
the trees tell lies windows listen
eyes all mute otherwise silence
the sound of my heart drunk again
staggering among strangers
less strange than friends

where there was never a first time
and now it is gone
what must be done will be done
but I don't know what to do without you
I have few words no one to tell them to

we are having the wonderful summer
of winter which goes on and on
forgive me my sins known and unknown
my pain the worst of them
your pain not the least

the language of this country
is not declined
nothing belongs to anything here
and *to come back* does not mean *to return*

IN THE BEGINNING WAS THE WORD

I can verify the story from Cain to Abel,
from the snake in the garden to the bloody sea.
I was there. I saw everything, knew everybody.
I knew about Potiphar's wife and kept my mouth shut.
I saw the frogs and lice and watched the firstborn die.
What could I do? I was sent to observe and report,
and I reported that the waters of Mara were bitter
and all the males of Midian were slain. I saw Jael
with her nail and hammer, and Bathsheba preparing
for her widowhood. I saw the heel of God
as he departed hastily, and I was not
blinded by it as the others were.

I saw it all repeated in the good news
and the bad news and the letters smuggled from prison.
I was there when Saul had a vision and repented.
And when Salome danced, I whistled and applauded.
I had my orders. I saw the plate they brought her.
I spoke to Lazarus in Paradise. That crazy beggar
refused me a drink of water. And when the crowd
outside the palace shouted for blood, I knew
they would be rewarded. They were.
And later I saw the lost apostle suffering
from something worse than fear. The poor fool
had been duped. He hanged himself. It is all true

exactly as I recorded it. It is disgusting,
intolerable, and it is all true.

THE STONE GARDEN

1

everything is quiet in the garden
there are statues
but no children

the husband stands
at the edge of the terrace
silhouetted against evening
like a chimney whose house has burned
looking across the stones
toward the trees

she leans back in a deck chair
and watches a bright cloud
dying in the east

then the first cool air
at the end of a long summer
passes over them
and for a moment they forget they possess
many things they no longer want
including each other

2

the wife sits all afternoon
beside the pool in the garden
reading a book with blank pages
less tedious than words

it is a murder mystery
and she reads carefully
even the margins

she does not care who committed the murder
but is eager to find out
how it was done

3

he is ill
and nausea arrives daily
to stand before him like a sycophant
making the sign of a fig

old friend the husband whispers
where do you spend the night that you can
be here so early each morning

beside his bed
is a vase of flowers
which came to him as strangers
with nothing but their leaves and petals
and the light to which they still turn
although dying

his eyes rove out the window
and wander through the stone garden
like lost sheep on a mountain
until the call of their bells
disappears in the fog

4

the widow has burned her book
and hidden its ashes under stones
in the garden

when she goes there
she is disturbed by the raucous voices
of thrashers and wrens
and by tiny lizards whose eyes
follow her everywhere

5

she has three pills left in the bottle
and each is a little silence
one the silence of rest
one the silence of sleep
and one the silence of death

have I come so far she says
that I should fear a little silence
and takes all three

she goes out and sits in the garden
pretending she is on a boat
moored at the edge of a broad river
and she hears small waves
whispering around her

one by one her fears
slip over the side of the boat
and swim across the river

when they emerge on the far shore
they are beautiful children
her beautiful children
with the sun already drying their hair

she sleeps and the stone boat
drifts out to sea

6

on stormy nights
he is a crazed face at the window
peering in from the stone garden

and sometimes when there is a moon
she can be seen standing by the pool
in a white dress
but at dawn she turns away
and leads her children across the water

evenings in autumn the two of them
walk barefoot through the garden
their feet are uncut by the stones
but the stones bleed
and the cold
licks at the edges of everything

then darkness thickens
and late birds hurtling toward home
are trapped in flight and suspended
calling down to their helpless trees

Shirley Kaufman, *The Floor Keeps Turning*
Shirley Kaufman, *From One Life to Another*
Shirley Kaufman, *Gold Country*
Ted Kooser, *Sure Signs: New and Selected Poems*
Larry Levis, *Wrecking Crew*
Jim Lindsey, *In Lieu of Mecca*
Tom Lowenstein, tr., *Eskimo Poems from Canada and Greenland*
Archibald MacLeish, *The Great American Fourth of July Parade*
Peter Meinke, *The Night Train and The Golden Bird*
Peter Meinke, *Trying to Surprise God*
Judith Minty, *In the Presence of Mothers*
James Moore, *The New Body*
Carol Muske, *Camouflage*
Leonard Nathan, *Dear Blood*
Leonard Nathan, *Holding Patterns*
Kathleen Norris, *The Middle of the World*
Sharon Olds, *Satan Says*
Gregory Pape, *Border Crossings*
Thomas Rabbitt, *Exile*
Ed Roberson, *Etai-Eken*
Ed Roberson, *When Thy King Is A Boy*
Eugene Ruggles, *The Lifeguard in the Snow*
Dennis Scott, *Uncle Time*
Herbert Scott, *Groceries*
Richard Shelton, *Of All the Dirty Words*
Richard Shelton, *Selected Poems, 1969-1981*
Richard Shelton, *You Can't Have Everything*
Gary Soto, *The Elements of San Joaquin*
Gary Soto, *The Tale of Sunlight*
Gary Soto, *Where Sparrows Work Hard*
David Steingass, *American Handbook*
Tomas Tranströmer, *Windows & Stones: Selected Poems*
Alberta T. Turner, *Learning to Count*
Alberta T. Turner, *Lid and Spoon*
Chase Twichell, *Northern Spy*
Constance Urdang, *The Lone Woman and Others*
Cary Waterman, *The Salamander Migration and Other Poems*
Bruce Weigl, *A Romance*
David P. Young, *The Names of a Hare in English*
David P. Young, *Sweating Out the Winter*